The Power Of The "P"

The Principle P's to Productive, Prosperous, & Purposeful Living

Tracey Armstrong

The POWER of the P's

The Principle P's to Productive, Prosperous, & Purposeful Living

Copyright © 2023 by Trient Press

All rights reserved. No part of this publication may be reproduced, distributed, or transmitted in any form or by any means, including photocopying, recording, or other electronic or mechanical methods, without the prior written permission of the publisher, except in the case of brief quotations embodied in critical reviews and certain other noncommercial uses permitted by copyright law. For permission requests, write to the publisher, addressed "Attention: Permissions Coordinator," at the address below.

Criminal copyright infringement, including infringement without monetary gain, is investigated by the FBI and is punishable by up to five years in federal prison and a fine of $250,000.

Except for the original story material written by the author, all songs, song titles, and lyrics mentioned in the novel The POWER of the P's are the exclusive property of the respective artists, songwriters, and copyright holder.

Trient Press
3375 S Rainbow Blvd
#81710, SMB 13135
Las Vegas,NV 89180

Ordering Information:
Quantity sales. Special discounts are available on quantity purchases by corporations, associations, and others. For details, contact the publisher at the address above.
Orders by U.S. trade bookstores and wholesalers. Please contact Trient Press: Tel: (775) 996-3844; or visit www.trientpress.com.

Printed in the United States of America

Publisher's Cataloging-in-Publication data
Armstrong, Tracey
A title of a book : The POWER of the P's
ISBN
Paper Back   979-8-88990-073-3
Ebook   979-8-88990-074-0

DO YOU REALLY want a Productive and Prosperous Life?
DO YOU REALLY want to press past your PAST?
DO YOU REALLY want a brighter FUTURE?
If You do, then this book is for you.

Living a Productive Life is the measurement of a person's progress toward their significant goals.

Living a Prosperous Life is about more than just money. It describes people who have achieved success in terms of wealth, health, and happiness. But it can also be used broadly, much like the words successful, thriving, and flourishing.

Prosperous is based on the verb prosper, which means to be successful.

Living a Purposeful Life Your life's vision defines who you want to be, what you want to be known for and the set of experiences and accomplishments you aim for. Your vision helps define the goals by giving you a framework to evaluate those goals.

Introduction-

When you realize that it is truly you holding yourself back from experiencing a better life then you will start to understand the Power of the P's. These P's will guide you to checking, changing, and controlling your mindset, emotions, and your actions. When these are under control, you will have a different result in life. Your impact and behaviors will be different. You will move differently and believe differently because you will now know how to live a purpose filled life that can lead you to a more productive and prosperous life. Your perspective is key to living a better life. If you want to change your life, you need to change the way you look at it. You need to find a new perspective. This might mean a change in your attitude and mindset the way you think of yourself. Many times we think of ourselves based on our past experiences and based on what others have said to us or about us. It has been those people and words that have crafted our perspective of what we can do, be, and experience. If people made us believe that we were not worthy of living an exceptional life then that is what we did. We lived life at the level of what others told us or believed in us. The experiences that happened to us in the past may have caused you to feel ashamed and inferior to those around you, but those experiences do not define you as a person. You should learn from the past and improve from those lessons. Those lessons are there to guide us into being the best version of ourselves.

P- Perspective of Yourself

If you want to change your life and improve your happiness the first step on the road of change is changing your perspective. Your Perspective is so powerful that it made it to the number one spot. Your PERSPECTIVE of SELF is so powerful that it will propel your life to another level of imprisoning your life to never excel. Your perspective of yourself means, how do you view yourself. How do you see yourself when it comes to what you can do, and what you cannot do? Do you believe that you can achieve the goals that you set out for, or do you not believe in yourself?

These are the first questions you need to ask yourself. If you don't check, change, and control your own perspective of yourself then you will never see the best version of yourself.

I remember, as an educator for many years, I have met so many students that have expressed how they do not see themselves as valuable and how they don't see any hope for the future Now, mind you, these are 11/12 year olds that are already feeling defeated in life. I always ask them where this perspective came from, and at such a young age why do they already feel hopeless. "I remember talking to a student, and she said, Ms. Armstrong, you are teaching us all this positive living information, but when we get home it goes right out the door. My mom tells me that I will never be anything" It was then that I realized, it was the lives of the parents and guardians that made them view themselves like they did. I was determined after that day, to always provide a glimpse of hope for anyone that I came in contact with. No matter if it was a student or a parent, I want you to know that there is hope after going through the pain and hurts from the past.

So, I continued to teach Perspective and how to change life for the better, no matter what anyone has told you about yourself, always ask yourself what do you think about your own life. It starts with your thoughts, leads to your emotions, displayed through your behavior, and manifests with your consequences and outcomes.

So, let's walk through this, every thought that enters the mind has only two outcomes for your life, either positive or negative. So, if the thought is a negative thought and you allow it to fester and grow in your mind then it will show in your emotions. Your emotions are always triggered by the thought of something.

Sometimes, nothing even has to happen, it could be you just thinking it is going to happen and you start to feel a certain way. These thoughts will create the emotion that matches your mindset. Therefore, negative emotions usually are revealed in the form of anger or sadness. Anger is the emotion that usually is revealed the most in those that think negative thoughts more frequently. The perspective of these people is that they have anger issues and that's just how they are. If you are always getting angry, where does that get you? Most people who are angry often are not happy. They usually act out in a violent manner, and they have behaviors that match their anger. If this is your perspective of yourself or you know someone that has the same perspective, then you completely understand this example. Once you or someone you know is angered, how do they respond? They will usually be outraged and fly off the handle with any remarks that are made. Otherwise, they will act out in an aggressive manner with physical force. When this happens we do not typically see a clear perspective of what is actually happening. If anger consumes your life more than any other emotion, the question you need to ask yourself is why? Why do you get angry so easily, what causes you to be triggered ubruptly?

Ways to Control Your Perspective-

-Stop comparing yourself to others:

When you compare yourself to others this is a way to bring yourself down to devalue yourself. It is a waste of time because you are comparing yourself to someone who has different talents and who has different strengths in different ways of living their life. Most of the time you don't see or know what that person is going through.

I remember wanting to be married. I wanted the life that some of my friends had with the husband and the big house. Now, it wasn't a sense of jealousy, but more of a I want that. Not knowing what was going on behind closed doors. The cheating and the abuse that could not be seen from the outside looking in. So, be careful what you allow to control your thoughts of yourself. "You may be wanting something that you really don't want. So be careful who you are wishing to be like because you never know what being them really consist of. Think about some of the celebrities that we see performing in the media and making it look as though they have it all together. They may have a smile on the outside, but within, they may be sad, unhappy, and depressed. You would think, why? They should be loving life, you may say, if it was me, I would be living it up. But you can't see what they have going on personally.

Many celebrities deal with mental health issues due to the stress of fame. The status may appear shiny and glittering on the outside, and that's what they want you to see. Most people will not go around telling you how bad it is. Especially if you grew up in a house where you were not allowed to talk about anything outside of the house. "What happens in this house stays in this house" was the motto for many children growing up, and it still is for some people today. So remember, what glitters is not always gold. This quote is one that I heard so many times as a child, but I never knew exactly what it meant until I started to really look at other things that may be shiny and they are not gold. So, with all of this remember don't judge yourself based on what you see another person showing you.

-Don't be so hard on yourself:

You are your biggest enemy and you are harder on yourself than anyone. You must stop criticizing everything that you do. You must learn to love yourself and give yourself a break. We beat ourselves up over small things which causes us to not pursue large things because we will judge ourselves and think that that is the same way that other people will judge us.

I remember when I first started my tumbling business. I didn't even call it a business because it wasn't as big as others, I would judge my small team and not think of myself as a real gym. It was in 2016, in Gene Green park, I started teaching cheerleaders from my little league team how to tumble and parents were paying me. I had my four mats from Academy, they were $35 each, and I taught them with all my heart. Random people would see me and ask if I could train their child. The classes began to grow, and I still judged myself saying how I needmore, it's not good enough. Now, I was pushing myself to be better andto achieve more, but it was how I did it that needed to change. I would go to the gym down the street and see what equipment they had and talk down on myself. I started ordering more mats, inclines, and octagons.

Now, I felt a little better, but I was still outside in a park. I started complaining about that. I put myself and my business down until we moved into a building in 2016.

You would have thought that now I would be happy and stop criticizing my gym. Instead, there was a new complaint. I would say, this building is raggedy. The parking lot would flood, and the insulation could be seen. I still put myself down, so I had to order more and do more, I still wasn't good enough for myself. Although new people were coming, and business was increasing. The clients doubled, then tripled, until I had a waiting list for people to get into the tumbling classes. People would constantly tell me that I was successful at what I was doing, but me being my biggest enemy could not see it. The gym that I kept comparing myself to actually lost a few of their athletes to my gym and that was major. It wasn't until a parent told me one practice how much of an impact my coaching had on her life. Because now, I wasn't only teaching tumbling, I had created an All-Star Competitive Cheer Team that traveled throughout the state competing. This parent opened my eyes to see that it wasn't about the size of the building, but the quality of what the athletes were getting when they came. I was judging myself based on what I thought would be important to them, and they had to remind me of what it really was about. So, if you are someone that judges yourself to the point where you lose focus of the big picture. You can encourage yourself to go after more, but you don't want to downgrade your value to the point that you can't see your success.

-Believe in yourself:

Believing is finding something as true, genuine, or real. When we believe in ourselves, we accomplish so many more goals than we ever expected we would. Have faith in yourself and don't give up on your dreams. The reason why believing in yourself is so powerful is because if you don't you won't even try. When you understand that belief ignites the motion. Think about it, if a basketball player doesn't believe they can dunk, chances are they won't even try to dunk. If you don't believe you can start your own business, you aren't even going to try to start. Our belief starts from our perspectives of ourselves. Your perspective is your belief of what you think you can do and what you think you can't.

I remember when I wanted to become a model. I was young and ambitious. I wanted to be a model before Top Model even came out. However, I was 5'2, dark-skinned, gap-toothed, with short nappy hair. There were no models that looked like me, so I didn't believe I would ever achieve that dream. I would practice my runway walk and stand, and dream of the day of being on the stage, but I never attempted because of my belief. When I graduated and went to college, I worked out more, my body was on point. I colored and straightened my hair, changed my look, and wore heels ALL the time. I now believed in myself. With that belief, I changed my actions. Instead of just dreaming, I started researching how to become a model. I entered beauty pageants and did more to move closer to that dream. I still had my gap, I still was dark, I still was short, but the only thing that changed was my belief in what I could do. All my practicing didn't go to waste, I walked multiple runways for a variety of pageants, I even got Top 3 in the Miss Teen Texas Beauty Pageant. This just goes to show that believing in yourself will take you to another level of your life.

-Realize that you can change it:

Perspective is situational. The way you view life depends on your situation. Your thoughts and mindsets are developed based on the situation you have gone through and overcome. Your perspective can control your thoughts if you only have a narrow way of looking at situations. Sometimes changing your views will change your thoughts and improve your mindset. It is when you improve your mindset of yourself that your life starts to blossom and open up. Your mindset will determine if you will go after your dreams and goals, or just settle for what has been given to you.

So, we think negatively of ourselves, but we don't want others to think negatively of us. It is you versus you and sometimes you must tell your mind to be quiet and to stop letting the doubts hinder your future. Your future begins with how you perceive who you are and what you are capable of doing.

P- Purpose & Passion

Live your life with purpose. Purposeful living will make you happier in life. When you follow your purpose prosperity will come. The power of having a purpose in your life is so enormous because it gives you your why. If you have an ultimate purpose then you have something that is you driving your efforts to succeed. My purpose is to have a positive impact on the people's lives that I come in contact with via in person or through social media.

I remember...... In 2015, I attended the Maximized Life Bible Training Institute offered at my church. During the class, the teacher taught me about finding and fulfilling our purposes in life. She explained how life without a purpose is a life without direction. When you learn what your purpose is in life, and you start going after it then your life will change. So, I was a Store Manager for a really profitable Starbucks store, I was the number one in charge. I was making money with my salary and bonuses, can't forget the free coffee everyday. I was enjoying my life serving people while serving coffee.

Customer service was my niche. Then it began to change simultaneously while I was in the class, the company started pushing the service to the backend and this was not what I had signed up for. I was discovering my purpose more in the class. I was also in a Faith class, so when you put Faith lessons, Purpose Lessons, and work challenges in the mix my thoughts about what I was doing with my life began to change, my purpose for life began to become more clear. I made a decision in February of 2015, after being in Management for 15 years, at the age 36, I stepped out on Faith and made the decision to leave Starbucks. Leave Management all together. I didn't have another job lined up for me, but I did have faith that I would find my place where I could flow in my purpose.

My purpose pushed me into teaching and helping to have an impact on our future generations. Of all careers, teaching, one of the lowest paying, underappreciated careers in the world. I didn't have a Teaching Certification because my degree was in Business management. I had to spend money to go back to school for that, and It wasn't easy when it came to finances. I moved out of my house and moved in with my aunt. I cashed out my 401K to ensure my living expenses were taken care of. I picked up small jobs while going through this transition. I never lost faith that I would achieve my goals and walk in my purpose. From March to July, I was studying, testing, and going after what I desired.

August 2015, I took the Teacher Certification and passed on the first try. When you start walking in your purpose, you will see some situations start to fall in line, and things will begin happening for you with little to no effort. The next week, I got a call for an interview at a school that I had not even applied to. The administrator told me that the Teacher Certification School sent them my scores, and I was highly recommended by them. I scheduled an interview for the next morning. After the interview, I had not made it home yet, and I was given an offer to become a Full-Time Educator at a school that was only 5 mins from where I was living. When I tell you that the trials that I had been facing after leaving Starbucks all faded away. My focus was on having a positive impact on the lives of my students, even though I took a financial loss of almost $30K. I didn't let it bother me because I was fulfilling my purpose, and I had no lack even with the loss. Remember to find your purpose and prosperity will follow. Let's find yours.

-Discovering your Purpose:

If you have already discovered your purpose in life, good for you. Always remember to resort back to your purpose, especially when times get hard. Reflecting on the reason why you are on this earth will keep you pushing and pursuing your purpose. Many of you may not know your purpose. Most people will ask at some point of their lives, "Why am I here?" "What is my Purpose in life?" Many people still don't know. So many people live life without ever discovering their purpose. When you live a life with no purpose, that is what it means to just exist. Existing is being a part of something, but not really having any impacts or effects on anything. Don't just exist, Live Life to the fullest. This to me means living life with purpose which makes life so much worth living. Everyone has a purpose in life, you are created with purpose within, but until you tap into it then you will never walk it out in life. That's what it means by living a purposeful life.

Your purpose in life is as unique to you as your fingerprint. We all have a particular set of talents, experiences, skill sets, and interests that light us up. Purpose is related to these, but it is your reason for being. It is why you get out of bed in the morning, even when the day is dreary, you're tired, and you know the tasks and challenges ahead are going to be hard or even boring. It's like your passion. Start with thinking about what you are passionate about. What do you enjoy doing? What makes you smile? Then, think about how you can provide that to others because purpose is usually tied together with serving others. Your purpose may shift as life shifts. Your feeling of purpose may come from connections to others. So to help you discover your purpose here are a few tips:

Develop a growth mindset- Having a growth mindset is linked to having a sense of purpose. Constantly growing and becoming a better version of yourself helps you identify your purpose and commit to pursuing it.

Create a personal vision statement- A personal vision statement can help you manage stress and find balance in your life. It also serves as a roadmap that will guide you toward your purpose by identifying your core values and establishing what's important to you.

Explore your passions- Your passions and interests are a good indicator of the area in which your life purpose might lie. But they can be hard to identify. They're so ingrained in our ways of thinking that we can become blind to them. If you're not sure what your passions are, ask the people who know you best. Likely, you're already pursuing them in some way without even realizing it.

Turn your pain into purpose- We all face struggles in life. Overcoming these challenges shapes who we become and gives us our unique strengths and perspectives. Many people ask for help when struggling to overcome a major life change. Some later find their purpose in helping others facing similar struggles to those they have overcome.

Step number four is what I have done. Turning the painful experiences into life lessons that can help others overcome any obstacles that they may be facing. The trials and tribulations of your life that you have overcome can help others with similar situations have strength to overcome. As an educator, I am able to encourage my students through the tough situations of life with parents, peers, and pressures that they face especially in middle school.

I remember telling them about the pain of middle school that I experienced. While in 6th grade, I hated myself. I hated the way I looked, I hated my life. My father was in and out of jail. My mother was very strict and demanding. To make matters worse, other classmates would talk about me, laugh at me, and make me feel like less than. This hurt my self-esteem and caused me not to believe in myself. I was super smart, but whenever I tried to show it, students would call me names. I never understood why. I still don't. I remember comparing myself to this other student and not liking her because I thought she was so pretty. She was tall, had long hair, and had a light-skin tone. She never did anything to me, but I didn't like her because all the boys did. I guess I was jealous back then. After I got to know her, she wasn't too bad of a friend. Found out that she didn't like being tall, she didn't like all the attention from the boys, she didn't like parts of herself that I thought were bonuses.

When I tell this story to my students, I instantly am walking in my purpose because I am taking what I went through and helping my students understand how to get through the same situation. They can relate to what I went through in one way or the other. I usually have some type of impact on their lives and that is my purpose in life. They will understand better how to navigate through some of the toughest years of their lives. Seeing their faces, when I tell them that they are not alone, and hearing the responses of shock to know that their teacher, a successful-college educated woman experienced bullying, low-esteem, and self-hate. Yes, I did, but I rose above it. This is a demonstration to them that they can too.

Once I realized that my pain can help, I stopped trying to bury it. This is where a lot of your purpose may stem from. Behind every successful person is clarity of purpose. And unless you find yours, you'll continue to cruise through life on autopilot. You may find yourself knocked off-course and lost, uncertain how to move forward or which direction is forward. Or, life may be smooth but one day you may look back and wish you had used your time differently. When you do discover your purpose, It requires some courage because it opens up questions and ideas that might not be comfortable. Purpose provides you with an inner compass that guides every decision and leads you to the experiences that will light up your life. Then you act differently.

I remember when my purpose started to become clear to me. I started living life differently. When you live a life of purpose, you focus on different things in your life. You care about people differently. Every move you make is intentional because you have a purpose attached to it. Some family and friends could not understand what I was doing, why I was changing. I had a different mindset. I was working toward something that they could not see or understand. Especially, when I changed careers and took a financial loss.

They could not understand why I would do that. I recall my mother saying, "Why are you throwing your life away?" You may have some people in your life that may feel the same way. But remember, this is your life and you are the only one that can live it. I was intentional of how I spent my time, I was intentional of who I spent my time with. This was important because if I would have continued spending my life clubbing, partying, and drinking. I would have never been able to walk in my purpose.

For you, it will all depend on what you are called to do in the world. Some are listed below, but it must be one that you truly care about:

-Helping Children, Giving Back to the Community, Helping Animals, Helping Others Live a Healthy Lifestyle, Embracing Spirituality, Empowering Others Cultivating Healthy, Reciprocal Relationships My Passion was helping young people live a more hopeful life. Then my purpose expanded into my cheer gym, and the motto was "developing prosperous athletes on and off the mat." My purpose has expanded even broader to social media platforms in an effort to have a positive impact on more listeners. So your purpose may stay the same, but your platform may change as you develop and live life on purpose. Every action you make and every step you take, should have an intent behind whatever you do. If you do things and you do not have any intention for it. It will find an intention that you may not have planned for whether positive or negative. You're more likely to achieve goals and be happier and more content when you achieve what you were intending to achieve. Especially if it's your passion and your purpose, then prosperity will come.

P-Preparing for the Process

Now that you have checked and changed your perspective of yourself & discovered your purpose for living, it is time to prepare for the process. You may say the process of what? The process of purposeful living towards a more productive and prosperous life. One of my mentors, Phil Sorentino, would always remind me that "It's not an event; it's a process.' What this meant was that achieving your dreams doesn't just happen overnight. It is a process, and you need to prepare to go through it. It is the journey we call life. When preparing, it is going to require change. You must embrace the change in order to fully prepare. If you resist change and don't allow the process to take place, how will you ever grow?

Think about a plant, a plant starts off as seed that is planted. It is usually small round or oval shaped, different colors depending on what you are growing. After the seed is planted, it begins to change its perspective. It is no longer just a seed it starts to transform into a main root. It is no longer perceived as a seed. The main root forms and discovers its purpose. The purpose is to be the anchor of the plant, to hold it down. It also serves the purpose of absorbing food and water. If the main root doesn't fulfill its purpose then the plant doesn't live life to the fullest. It may survive, but it is not healthy. Think about it, in order for that seed to grow and develop it had to undergo a change. It had to change into that main root in order to serve its purpose. Change is necessary in life in order to live a productive and prosperous life.

You are the seed. In order for you to live a purpose filled life you must change your perspective of what you were, and become what God has purposed you to be. Just like a plant, you must find the right soil to be planted in. This can be correlated to the people you surround yourself with. If you surround yourself with groups that don't serve your purpose it's like a seed being planted in infertile ground. Also like the plant, you must nourish and value what you were created for. Your purpose is
like the main root. Feed it with the proper nutrients to help it grow. Provide yourself with plenty of water, so that you don't thirst. Thirst meaning having the feeling of a need not being met. When you surround yourself with the right people then they will support your changes.

Don't be like the plants that never grow and take root. The main root must be the anchor for the plant, you must anchor yourself in what you desire to be and prepare to undergo the process of changing.

Change is hard for a lot of people. But in order to have a better future you must be able to change your Viewpoint, change the way you think about situations, change the way you think about yourself, and change the way you think about the past. Let's look at some ways to prepare yourself for the process of changing your life.

Ways to prepare yourself:

Decide to Change
This is the first way to prepare because you have to make the decision that this is what you want to do. You want to live a more productive and prosperous life. Your decision will bring about some discomfort not just in your life, but the lives of those that surround you. Your decision to change must come from your heart. If you waffle on whether or not you are going to do it, then chances are more likely that you won't. It's like someone saying enough is enough. SInce you are reading this book, I can guess that you are at least thinking about the change. Which is a wonderful first step.

Learn to embrace Discomfort

Who likes discomfort? No one, and I am telling you to learn to embrace it. DIscomfort is the feeling of unease, anxiousness, and sometimes embarrassment. This is a part of the process. Preparing for the unease is important because when you step out to achieve a goal that you have never done before it won't always be easy. You may have to cry sometimes, but in the end it is worth it. You may have some growing pains, and that is a part of the process also. The feeling of anxiousness comes from not knowing what is going to happen. You must prepare your mind to be okay with not knowing all of the steps to get you to the life you desire, but if you keep on taking them you will eventually get there. The embarrassment may come when you don't know exactly what you're doing and others are watching and you feel awkwardness in your pursuit of a change. You must get past what you think people are thinking about you. Usually the ones that will have something to say are the same ones that are not making any moves themselves because people making moves already understand exactly what you are going through and they don't have time to be messing with you.

Stop Making Excuses

Some may say, " I don't make excuses, I give reasons why I can't do it". To make it clear, the definition of an excuse means a reason that tries to justify someone's fault or offense. This means that when you give your reasons why you can't start your business, you are actually making excuses. When you give your reasons why you can't live a prosperous life, you're making excuses. Sounds like your excuses are holding up your preparation. If you continually make excuses as to why you can't have what you desire, then why do you even desire anything. Do you only desire things that you know you can have? If so, then don't expect anything greater than what you have, or what you think you can have.

I remember making excuses for why I didn't start my Podcast. I didn't know exactly what a Podcast was? I didn't know all the steps in starting a podcast. I didn't understand what elements went into the creation of a podcast. These were my excuses for not moving forward. Guess what, all of the excuses I was making had answers to them. I had to make up my mind that I was going to stop making excuses and find the answers to achieve my goal. I did what I needed to do and was successful. If I would have kept making excuses about what I couldn't do in my life, I would have achieved as many goals that I have in my life.

Identify What is Holding You back

What's holding you back? Once you get rid of the excuses, really take a moment to think about what could actually be holding you back. You may say, you don't know what to do, so lack of knowledge can be temporarily holding you back. Lack of finances may be another obstacle, or lack of support from people. These are viable resources that could possibly be temporarily holding you back. As for finances, if this is an obstacle then instead of giving up and saying I don't have the money. You can try to find ways to make it happen. If you don't have the support of people, then you must learn to be your own support system sometimes.

I remember when my daughter was selected to perform in the Macy's Thanksgiving Day Parade in New York City. This was a dream come true. However, it was up to me to provide the finances for not just her to go, but for me also. I dare not send my child to New York at 15 by herself. SO the cost was doubled. I didn't have the money or much motivational support. Some of my family would say to us, that's too much money. She doesn't need to be going up there anyways. Some would express how, if we didn't have the money why are we even trying to do this. It wasn't a necessity. With these words being said to us, instead of me agreeing with them. I was determined, I had to be my own support system for the both of us. I create ways to generate funds. We did fundraisers, marketing campaigns, and whatever money making activities we could. I did not let the lack of finances or moral support stop me from achieving the goal I set out for. But you must prepare your mind to push past the list of things that will stop you.

Define the changes you want to make in your life

What changes do you want to make? Better Question, what changes do you need to make? When you are preparing to make changes, after identifying what's slowing you down, define what you want. Some people usually use tools like vision boards to define what they want. Sometimes you must start with some easy changes like your daily habits. Your daily habits can steal your time and energy without you even knowing.

I remember when I analyzed every hour of my day, and I noticed that I spent about 2-3 hours a day playing games on my phone. This was before my cheer gym. I realized I would spend so much time playing Candycrush and Tetris on my phone that it was an addiction. I would lose and have to keep playing until I won or fell asleep. Then, I would wake up in the morning and start my morning playing games and wasting time that could have been used toward achieving my goals. I had to make the change. When I kept making the excuse that I didn't have time in the day to do what I needed to do, I had to define what change would create more time in my life. Deleting those games from my phone increased my productivity dramatically. The time I was wasting in the morning was reallocated to research business needs and checking emails in the morning instead of gaming. This was one of the best changes that I decided to make. When defining the changes you want, look at your excuses and what's holding you back, and then set some goals.

Set SMART Goals

You may ask what SMART goals are. They are an Essential part of preparing for the process. Every business uses the acronym to explain the type of goals that need to be set. S.M.A.R.T. means: SPECIFIC. MEASUREABLE. ATTAINABLE. RELEVANT.
TIME-BASED

Once you have defined what you want to change, these goals have goals. Every goal should be specific.
   -Specific to what you desire, no room for misinterpretation, nor confusion.
   -Measurable goals can be tracked. You can actually determine whether or not you are making progress on your goal.
   -Attainable goals should be able to be achieved with time and effort if you can meet them.
   -Relevant goals should line-up with your overall dreams and purpose. If the goal doesn't relate to what you're trying to achieve, why is it on your list?
   -Time-based goals have a target date for completion. EVen if it's due dates throughout the process, to keep you moving forward and not becoming stagnate.

   Setting these types of goals will help you prepare for going through the process. Put this together, and you're left with a detailed goal-setting plan that keeps you focused and headed in the right direction. Using the SMART goal framework helps to direct your actions so that they all contribute to reaching your goals. As you implement this framework, it may highlight where you could run into challenges. That allows you to plan and chart a detailed course prepared for obstacles.

   Developing an action plan that works for you can be difficult.

   I remember managing for the JCPenney Corporation, and using the framework was crucial to completion of tasks and major events. We would sit in the Management meetings and breakdown every upcoming event and plan using SMART goals. For instance, when it came to an event like Black Friday, we had to have every i dotted and every t crossed to be profitable. We would plan specific dates, times, inventory, staffing needs, and customer needs. Then we would have measurable sales goals based on the trends and marketing. We would create an overall attainable goal based on the previous year's sales, and this year's projections. At the same time, we would create a stretch goal that was more than the attainable goal, but if we planned properly we had a chance of reaching our stretch goal. This was always necessary because even if we didn't meet the stretch goal, we made the attainable goal and everyone would make money. Then the goals were relevant to the particular event. If we were planning Black Friday, we were not thinking of Summertime goals because they were not relevant to what we were trying to achieve. After completing the various moving parts, we would put a Time-frame to the project. Each department had its own time frames. Stock Replenishment had different timeframes from the Pricing team, because the timeframes depended on the task required.

So, whenever you create your own SMART goals remember that all goals do not have to have the same time frames. Some may take longer than others, so always schedule multiple dates and times to achieve change because some take longer than others.

Create a Routine-

Prepare for the process by creating a daily routine. A sequence of actions that you regularly follow. When you have a routine it helps to keep track of your life and the progress of your change. The routine is how you operate and move in your purpose. When you have a routine, it saves you time and helps you change more quickly. Habits are formed in 21 days, so when you make your changes a regular part of your routine then they will become habits before you know it.

I remember this was one of the main lessons we learned as educators. Create a routine for your students. So, I have a routine for entering the classroom, and leaving the classroom. Students know what to expect and if the routine changes it actually causes them to be confused.

Every morning, I have a routine for getting myself and my class ready for the day. As they come into the room, there is an assignment on the board. They sharpen pencils, plug up laptops, and begin the assignment on the board. I take the first 5 minutes to take attendance while they finish the Bell Work. I then greet them and ask them how their day is going. If I do not do this at the beginning of class, a student will ask me if I am okay because it is a routine. When a student doesn't follow the routine, then I ask them if everything is okay with them because there is an expectation to follow the routine. Usually, if the student or I get off track, there is usually something happening within.

Routines give you a checklist for yourself that can gauge your productivity. When you are off track, you will be aware and get yourself back on track. With no routine, your life kind of drifts as the winds blow. Like my class would be, if I did not have a routine in place when they entered there would be students drifting and not being productive.

Exercise/Eat Right/Evaluate Your Health-

You may ask why you need to exercise in order to prepare for the process. If you don't take care of yourself, who else is going to take care of you? You cannot take care of others if you are struggling on yourself. So take care of the way you look at yourself, take care of the way you perceive your thoughts, take care of the way you handle your health. If you are not healthy, how can you be wealthy because you're not going to have the strength and the ability to do the things that you need to do. Your perspective of sleep should be that you need it. It is the way and the time for your mind to reset, refresh and restart. It is just like a battery, batteries need charging in order to work properly. When you charge them, they must sit still and be at rest and that is why your sleep is so important.

Eating a balanced diet is also important because your food is like the gas in the car, if you feed your car bad gas, it is going to cause your car to act up. The same as your body, if you're putting only bad things into your body, eventually your body is going to not be able to function and it will also begin to act up. Exercise is important in taking care of yourself because like a car if a car sits still for too long the battery will be drained or parts will start to rust. A car must be driven regularly in order for all of the parts of the car to operate as they were designed and built to do. If it is not moving for long enough then that belt will start to rot, and when you do want to drive that car the belt may pop and break because it has not been used. The oil hasn't been flowing through it just like your body. When your body doesn't move, or you do not exercise, the parts of your body do not function properly like it should.

I remember when I did not properly take care of my health. I was going every day, all day. I had school, teaching from 8a-4p, school cheer practice from 4p-6p, tumbling classes from 6:30p-9:30p, not leaving the gym until 10p or 11p some nights. This was Monday through Friday. On Saturday mornings, I had All-Star Cheer practice from 9a-1p sometimes 2 or 3 depending on competition season. Then I had my daughter's school activities also. On Sundays, I was a part of the Dance Ministry at church so, I had to be there on Sundays from 8a until 11a. I would rest from 12p-2:30p, because we then had practice from 3p-6p sometimes 8p on Sunday nights, depending on how well they performed. I ran myself ragged. I did this from 2016 to 2019.

It was in 2019, my body said no more. I had neglected my health because I didn't have time to go to the doctor. One night, my side was aching unbearably, it had been aching on and off all during the week. I spiked a fever. It was the highest I had ever had in my life. The next day I was rushed to the hospital with Severe Sepsis Shock. My body was shutting down, an infection was spreading to my organs, and my life was on the line. As a result, I stayed in the hospital for a week in pain and barely hanging on.

The point that I am driving home, is that me being in the hospital did not serve my purpose. I couldn't teach, coach, or live life. You need to prepare your mind as well as your body for the process of change. Change can be stressful, and stress takes a toll on your body. How can anyone be productive and live a prosperous life if they are stuck laid-up in a hospital.

Evaluate who is in your circle.

When preparing for the process, you want to get yourself together first, then get your team together. Evaluating your circle means to judge or calculate the quality, importance, amount, or value of some of the people that you surround yourself with. You may have to make your circle smaller to achieve your goals. First calculate the quality of each person. What qualities do they bring to your life? Are they the friend that pulls you back to where you came from? If so, they have to go. Judge the importance of each person. How important is it to have an entire entourage? Think about who you can call on in the time of need. They will help you figure out the level of importance. Calculate the amount of people you have in your circle and decide how important they are to remain and what are their qualities. Then think about the value that they add to your life. Do they help you or hinder you from walking in your purpose?

While it's easy to spot the toxic people you should immediately banish from your life, it can sometimes be more difficult to decide who you should invite into your life and keep close. Research has proven that the most successful people usually have an average of 5 friends. These are friends that will add different aspects of friendship to your life. Think about which friend you have that falls into these categories.

The leader: This is the person that always takes you to the edge of where you feel comfortable. They bring you to the brink of what you think you're capable of by simply pushing you to do more. They are unafraid to take charge, grab you by the hand, and go. You never feel less than perfectly capable.

The storyteller: This is the friend who colors your day with experiences from his or life. They inspire you to continue moving and trying for more adventure yourself.

Although we all know that complacency is the way to boredom, the storyteller reminds of how much more there can always be.

The listener: A person who stays with you to hear you out when you need a sounding board for your emotions is incredibly important. This is the friend that makes us feel valued even when we are unsure whether or not our words matter.

This isn't the person who will talk over you or just nod and text through your conversation. It's the person who really hears you, not just the person who listens.

The happy one: There's always someone we have in our life who fills us with iridescent, inexplicable joy simply from his or her presence alone. It's something practically chemical – something we honestly can't explain. Some people just honestly bring happiness with them, no matter where they are or whom they are with. Find this positive energy and hold on tightly to it.

The one who forces you to think: Although it's never a pleasant process to reevaluate our own lives, it can be necessary to check-in from time to time.

Self-reflection is necessary for any sort of improvement in our lives, no matter how trying it may feel at the moment. Sit down with the person who will ask you the right kind of questions to better who you are – and keep that person close.

I remember having a circle of about 12 friends that I hung out and partied with for nearly 20 years. We developed friendships beginning in Jr. High and lasting through High School and college. The group of friends grew as we met new people and had new experiences in life. When I started my gym shifted my time and energy that I would put into going out and chilling, I now focused my efforts to have a successful business and my purpose. After not attending a few of the birthday parties, the invitations begin to slow down. Eventually the invitations stopped, and when I did happen to hear about a gathering and attend, the first words I heard were, "well you're always busy" which was true, nevertheless, anytime I wasn't I made sure I showed up to be a support. After a few years, I got used to being left out of the invites and the level of friendships started to dwindle. I had to come to grips that I was no longer a part of the Crew the way I was in the past. I had to come to grips that I was no longer in the same space in my life, and I had changed. I wasn't the party animal that they knew me to be. So, when I did get invited to some events, I didn't even feel comfortable anymore in that atmosphere.

Sometimes, we will lose friends and you must prepare yourself for that experience because everyone is not going to understand why you have changed, and everyone is not going to support you. As you prepare for the process, evaluate yourself then evaluate your circle. Find your 3-5 that will be supportive and give you valuable input to assist you in moving toward the right direction and to not pull you back.

Simplify Your Life-

When you simplify your life you have more time & energy to focus on the things that really matter. So declutter yourself, declutter your home, declutter your mind because your mind gets rid of unnecessary obligations. When you rid your mind of items that are not geared towards your goals, then you can focus more on moving towards them. Your mind is like multiple file cabinets. Imagine an office space with file cabinets that are all open at the same time, and you have pulled multiple files out, and they are spread out on the desk. This is what your brain is like when it is cluttered with thoughts, ideas, and goals, but there's no organization. No game plan.

I remember watching a documentary of George Lucas and the creation of the movie Star Wars, one of the greatest action movies of all time. The animation and special effects were before its time. They explained how Lucas had so many thoughts in his mind on what he wanted and how he wanted it to be created. He had creators building model jets, and animated creatures left and right, but he did not prepare for the process of making it all come together. The workers were getting frustrated, it was like he had 100 file cabinet drawers open, with all of the files on the desk, on the floor everywhere. It wasn't until they brought in the person that helped to simplify the process by showing them how to storyboard. She gathered all of the people and showed them what to do with what they had, get rid of what they didn't need, and to organize so that everyone could understand what was happening. This is why simplification is important for preparation. Prosperity can not live in chaos.

    The process will be well worth it once you surpass any obstacles that will attempt to deter your focus. Therefore, preparing for this process of your life is a very important task and if you remember the ways to prepare for each new process you endeavor, you will make it through and you may not have to struggle as much because you've already prepared your mind and your body. Those that don't prepare are more likely to struggle more through the process.

P- Planning/Pursuit of prosperity

When you prepare for the process it makes the planning and pursuit of your prosperity a little easier. Not saying it will be easy, but some of the headaches can be dealt with before you start planning and pursuing. There are many quotes that describe the power of planning.
"A goal without a plan is just a wish"- Antoine de Saint-Expurey
"Plan your work and work your Plan"- Napoleon Hill
When establishing your goals, make a plan, write it down and make it clear. The plan is the roadmap for being more productive. Those who fail to plan, plan to fail.

There are several reasons why you should always plan before making a move.
-Planning Reduces Stress: the plan makes you and other people working with you more at ease because everyone is on the same page. When people are working in agreement, there is a better flow of progress. Lack of planning brings frustration and that brings division.

-Planning promotes Positivity: plans give comfort and bring joy to your life. Your plans determine your mood. Good planning makes you feel better about your pursuit. Poor planning makes you feel unprepared and lack of preparation brings negativity.

-Planning boosts productivity: you are not trying to figure out which way to go and which moves to make when you have a plan in place. You will get more done when you have a plan of direction for your pursuit.

-Planning helps you to meet your goals more expeditiously.
Now, a plan may not go as planned 100% of the way through. You may have to make adjustments to the plan, but that doesn't mean that the plan didn't work. An adjustment to a plan doesn't mean to throw the entire plan away which is what some people will do. Once you have developed your plan, now it's time to pursue your dreams.

Pursue means to hunt or chase. It's time to hunt down your goals. Chase after them until you reach them. When you begin to pursue your dreams, don't be afraid to try new things. The only way to achieve newness in life is by attempting new things.
Some people never experience anything new because they can't see themselves having bigger and better things. Also, some never

experience new things because of fear of failing or judgment. The what ifs kick in, what if this happens or what if I'm not successful? What if I fail? What if no one likes me? What if they laugh at me? What if they judge me? What if I am no good? What if I mess up? What about when they laughed at me 20 years ago? What about when my company did not succeed 10 years ago? What about when things didn't work out for me as I planned before? You are letting your past learned lessons harm your future because of what happened.

    Don't be afraid to fail. Failure is a part of life and if you never feel at anything how will you ever know how to win. The key to failing is learning from it when you fail. It is a lesson that should teach you how to do it better the next time, but what most people do when they fail they stop. It is just like when you fall down on a bike, and they say get back up and try again. For those that fall and don't get up, they never try and succeed at that particular test. However, those that fall and then get back up and try again will usually succeed once they learn from the mistakes they made and change what they did and then move on. The only way that you know that you will reach your goal is if you continue going after it long enough. Most people don't want to look like a fool or a failure, so some don't even try. How can you ever master a task if you never mess up and try again. The fear of failure has crippled so many people for so many generations that it gets passed down from generation to generation.

    Jordan Peterson-"If you're not willing to be a fool then you're not willing to be a master"

    When you begin your pursuit, as you chase your dreams, it's not really a chase, but when you head in the direction of it, it isn't moving further away from you, it is actually not moving at all. The more you move towards it, the faster you get to it.

    The more time, energy, and attention you give to a desired result. The law of attraction begins to work when you pursue your desires. What is the law of attraction? It states that whatever you focus your energy on will come back to you.

    By focusing on what you want to achieve, the law states that you'll emit positive energy to attract those achievements to you.

    I remember taking AP Physics in High School, I was such a nerd. But that nerdom paid off because a lot of life has to do with physics. So

I loved it.

Newton's laws of Motion are so relevant when it comes to pursuing. You may wonder, what does Newton have to do with your life? Think about this,

Newton's First Law of Motion (Inertia) States that an object at rest remains at rest, and an object in motion remains in motion at constant speed and in a straight line unless acted on by an unbalanced force. This is so true. You are the object. If you never move and stay in one place, you will never achieve your goals. When you begin to make moves, you will keep moving at the same speed unless something or someone gets in your way. That's the part that slows people down or stops them all together. You can not let someone that is not balanced with you force you off track.

What about, Newton's Second Law of Motion that says acceleration (gaining speed) happens when a force acts on a mass. When you put your force behind pursuing your prosperity, then your life gains speed and accelerates toward prosperity faster. This can be for anything you try to accomplish. The more force equalling your time, energy, & effort you give to a project the greater chance of completing the project sooner. Just like driving a car, the more you accelerate the faster the car goes, the faster the car goes, the faster you reach your destination. So, with this law, I learned that the faster I work toward my goals the faster I will achieve them.

The third law is what really causes people not to succeed. Newton's third law states that when two bodies interact, they apply forces to one another that are equal in magnitude and opposite in direction. The third law is also known as the law of action and reaction. Simply put, that for every action there is an equal and opposite reaction. Every step you take towards your goal will have a force pushing back at you. Every action you make will have an opposite reaction that may cause you to quit, but his law also says that if your force applied is greater than the force pushing against you, then you will overcome.

Your energy that you give to pursuing your prosperity must be greater than the negative energies that will push back at you. This also correlates to the Universal Law of Compensation, another restatement of the Law of Sowing and Reaping. It says that you will always be compensated for your efforts and for your contribution, whatever it is, however much or however little. So, if your efforts to achieve your goals are minimal then your results will be as well. If your efforts are massive to your pursuit, then your results will be greater.

Once you decide you want to change and live a more productive and prosperous life, These laws of the Universe will either work for you or work against you depending on how much you are willing to invest in yourself to plan and pursue your prosperity.

I remember when I thought about becoming a Motivational Speaker in 2019. I had the thought in my mind, but I was not putting much action behind my thoughts. During COVID year 2020, the world was shut down. All I had was time. We were all cooped up in the house for a few months. People were afraid to go anywhere. I closed the gym and wasn't coaching or teaching at the moment. That is when I started the book writing process. I had pages and pages of information that just flowed through me. Before then, I was too busy doing everything else that I never pursued what I dreamt of. This is how the Universe works, wherever I put my energy, I succeed. When I put my energy into Teaching, it came to me. When I put my energy into Coaching, the athletes came to me. When I finally decided to put more energy into speaking, the people and the platform that could help me launch my speaking career were sent to me. It wasn't until I put my Energy and Force behind my pursuits that made the Universe respond.

What are you wanting to pursue? Remember, the universe is waiting for you. What you reap you shall sow? Whether good, bad, or indifferent, it will come back to you one way or another. So, sow your TEA, Time, Energy, and Attention into your purpose to help you accelerate your Prosperity.

P- Positivity in Thinking & People

The way you think about life will bring the types of vibes and energy into your life. The energy you give is the energy you receive. The law of attraction is a philosophy suggesting that positive thoughts bring positive results into a person's life, while negative thoughts bring negative outcomes. This is the philosophy of life that has been proven time and time again. If you go into a situation thinking you are going to fail, chances are you will. Why? Because you never really believed therefore, you never really tried. It revisits the Power of Thought Loop. Your thoughts control your emotions, your emotions determine your actions, and your actions will have an outcome whether positive or negative. The thoughts you think will ultimately result in your outcome. Furthermore, having positive thoughts means to have confidence and hope for the future. These thoughts are necessary to live a more productive life.

When faced with difficult situations in life, trying to find the positive will catapult you towards a more desirable result. There will always be challenges that you will face in life, how you go through them is what will determine your success. If you choose to think negatively, you will not see the possible outcomes or lessons that can be learned while going through. When you display negative vibes, chances are your disposition is not constructive and your focus is on what is not present rather than what is. When you look for the bright side of the situation, chances are you will find it, but you are guaranteed to not find it if you never look.

I remember coaching my tumbling classes and telling my athletes how powerful their thoughts were. During one class, an athlete was working on her round-off back-handspring. She had learned all the drills and skills needed to complete the tumbling pass, but she had a mental block. A mental block is when your thoughts don't line up with your actions. As long as I was there to support and hold her up, she was able to do it. Her positive thoughts were confident, and she put forth the actions to achieve the goal.

Nevertheless, when I was not there to hold her up, her thoughts turned to negativity. She doubted herself and did not commit herself to completing the skills. I knew she could do it, she knew she could do it, but her thoughts kept telling her that she could not. It was not until she replaced those thoughts of negativity with those of I can, I will, I must which is a motto I teach all athletes to say as they perform a skill on their own. She would set up for the tumbling past, and I could hear her say out loud, I can, I will, I must then she completed the pass. I would initially be close to her, then back up more, and then she had it. She was so elated when she finally overcame the obstacle. The only way she overcame that obstacle was by changing the way she thought about what she could do.

    Positive states of mind have been shown to fuel incredible results in our life and work in a number of ways. Highly successful people take time to actively seek out thoughts and circumstances that put them into a positive state of mind. If you want to increase the amount of positive thinking & feeling in your life, researchers have found that you can do a few things each day that seem so basic as to make you wonder if they work. Some ways to assist in obtaining and maintaining positive thinking:
    -Do mindfulness exercises or meditate. The point is to bring calm and focus to your mind; and to reset the stressor chemical cortisol. Every day.
    -Keep a gratitude journal. Plenty of research shows that people who write down a simple statement of something that happened to them that day for which they are grateful.
    -Keep a file for things that warm your heart like YouTube videos or stories of people doing remarkable things. Visit those each day for a few minutes.

    Your Prosperity is tied to your thinking and mindset. Research has shown that in order to achieve more in life you must have a Growth Mindset. There's a Growth Mindset and Fixed Mindset, Growth Mindset is believing that with time and effort you can achieve your goals. On the other hand, with a fixed mindset, your thoughts are whether you are born with it or not. They believe that everything is fixed and thinking positive is foolish. For those that have a Growth Mindset, the thoughts are mostly positive with the hopes of achieving more than what they are born with. It describes a way of viewing challenges and setbacks. Although they struggle with certain skills, they want to grow their lives and their futures.

    Think about it, how can you be prosperous if you don't believe you can grow. We must first understand that being prosperous is more than having a lot of money. Prosperity is a mindset, a way of interacting in our lives, and a way of thinking. Mastering this train of thought is not easy, but it is simple enough if we keep working on it consistently. Here are some ideas to help you improve your thoughts, and ultimately attract more prosperity into your life:

-Use positive affirmations to begin training yourself to think positively. Use "I am" statements such as "I am worthy of all that is good." Write the statements down and repeat them nightly before bed. Over time, this will implant these thoughts into your subconscious mind, and you will begin to naturally believe them.

-Creative visualizations can help you achieve prosperity by determining what it is you wish to achieve and then thoroughly creating that image in your mind. This works in the same way affirmations do. Our subconscious will fill with images of prosperity, and eventually, these subconscious "truths" will manifest in the physical. "See" yourself as being prosperous, and you will become so.

-Encourage yourself with the belief that you can achieve great things. This could also be one of your affirmations but expand on it. If you know you can earn a certain salary, tell yourself you can earn more. Allow yourself to believe all things are possible, and you will gain the confidence needed to reach higher than you ever imagined you could. If you believe you can do it, you are more likely to take the risks associated with people who are highly successful. Prosperity and success go hand in hand, so take risks and aim higher.

The negative thoughts will come at you left and right. In a study, they showed that we have approximately 60,000 per day. Now, an average of 2,500 thoughts an hour. With so many thoughts, you have to learn how to control them. Recognizing which ones are beneficial for your future and the ones that are not must happen repeatedly. If you allow thoughts to fester in your mind that are not productive, they will eventually lead to an unproductive action. When the thoughts come, recognize them, then remove the thought from your mind. In order to remove the thoughts you may have to verbally express to yourself to not think those thoughts. Then replace the thoughts with a new thought that would better serve your ultimate purpose. Usually, it will be saying the reverse of the original thought.

Finally, Reset that new thought in your brain and focus on it.

Positive people are so powerful. The people in your life are so powerful. The words they speak to you, about you, or for you can make or break your day and your life. Positive people will help you see various perspectives of different situations.

Negative people will only see one. Having positive people in your life doesn't mean to have someone just agreeing with every decision you make. Being a positive person also doesn't mean having a smile on your face everyday and never facing any challenges. This means to surround yourself with people who will assist you on your way to living a more productive and prosperous life. While living a life of purpose, these people will remind you of your goals and help you stay focused on achieving your dreams. Positive people will make an attempt to solve problems and operate from the viewpoint of making a way. On the contrary, negative people will only try to bring you down because they are not able to see the end goals. They will make you feel like your efforts are in vain. They will be the naysayers that don't believe in your dreams. Those who don't think it is worth the time, energy, and effort, especially when a task gets difficult. Those negative thoughts usually lead to negative productivity. So, be careful who you allow in your circle, the ones you are closest to are the most influential thoughts you listen to. The circle you surround yourself with will have either positive, negative, or neutral vibes; the power of attraction will attract these into your life.

Research has shown that more prosperous people are shown to be more positive in the aspect of having a can-do attitude. The people around should be able to be trusted with your dreams because you can not, I repeat you can not tell everyone your dreams. Everyone will not understand and everyone will not support. Believe me I know from experience.

I remember surrounding myself with family; some of all thought processes. When I would go to visit some family members, I had to be cautious of what I said around certain members of the family, especially if I was planning on making a change in my life. I would go to the house, sit down, and be minding my own business and next thing you know, here comes the 20 questions. I had to learn how to navigate around my goals with my answers because one day I slipped up. I was telling my family how I was going to stop teaching and become a motivational speaker. I said I wasn't feeling teaching anymore, and I wanted a change. The attacks began, "why would you do something foolish like that?", "A motivational speaker, hah, how do you expect to do that?", "there she goes chasing another dream", "you better stick to what you know". These unsolicited comments flooded the room and then my mind. "Maybe they are right", "No ones going to listen to me", "What am I thinking?" " I am being foolish". Now these thoughts have filled my mind because of the people that I allowed in my ear. I truly started to believe that I couldn't do this. I started having doubts that I never had before. The words my family said to me had a major impact on my mindset. This slowed down my productivity and my prosperity. I now had to erase their words and replace them with words that will bring me back on track.

Maybe you can remember being around people that didn't believe in you. It may have been friends or family. Maybe that family member told you that you would never amount to anything or that you were good for nothing, or maybe it wasn't that major. It could have been a laugh or facial expression they made when you showed them or told them what your plans were. It may have started as a child and still affects you today. You may still have people who don't believe in you. These are the people you must distance yourself from. I didn't say cut them off, but you can not constantly allow the negative energy to slow down your progress. It takes too much extra time and energy to erase the negativity in your life.

Now those were the positive and the negative, some may have neutral people in your life. You may say, well what's wrong with being neutral. When a car is in neutral where does it go? Nowhere or wherever you push it. People who stay neutral usually give no support, suggestions, or advice for you one way or another. What does this person bring to the relationship? They may be a sounding-board for you to release your thoughts, but they won't help with producing the thoughts. Not to say, to push the neutral people out of your life; however, you need to be aware of who they are and what their purpose is in your journey. They are not the advice givers, and they really won't be the support unless you request it.

Remember me telling you about the group of friends that I had at one point of time in life. Our friendship circle grew bigger and bigger as life progressed. The circle may have gotten bigger, but the connections were getting smaller. During these times of life, I was beginning my cheer business. I had a circle where I had to know who served which purpose. Out of the entire group, I would say two of the members were positive. They supported my dreams. They came out and promoted my business. Whenever we had events, I would invite the entire group, but I knew that those two would be there if they could. Now, why out of twelve people would only two support. I would always ask myself that question. I had to realize that just because we were in the circle together, didn't mean we had the same purpose in the circle. Some were probably the negative energy that doubted or judged in silence, and of course, the neutral people that swayed according to which friend they were hanging closest with. If they were with a positive friend, they would speak in high regards for my success. If they were around the negative people, they would swing the other direction. Now looking back on these situations, I can see who served which purpose in my life.

Sometimes, the people that may bring the most positivity into your life will be those who don't know you and don't know your past. These are the ones that actually allow you the opportunity to grow and to be the person you are aspiring to be.

Sometimes those that know you from the past, only know what you used to be and never allow you to be anything more. This is why they are sometimes the most negative people to be around. If they can only see the old you, how can they support you to be the new you. As you strive for a more productive, prosperous, and purposeful life you need to find some people that will give you the strength to soar and not drain your energy.

I also remember having strangers that did not know me support me more than those that knew me. I was coaching recreational cheerleading. The team had grown from a few athletes to over forty athletes in a few seasons. That is a lot of athletes on one cheer team. I gained the trust of these people that never met me, but they had heard that I was a good coach. They supported my vision for the team. I had friends that had girls they were putting in cheerleading, and they decided to put their athletes on other teams. I was shocked, but I had to understand that everyone won't be the people that are for you.

Once you understand the right people to have in your circle, you will be much more productive in your life. You can not gain success without people. People are necessary, but the right people are imperative. The wrong people will destroy everything that you work for. So, you must discern who has your back and who's stabbing you in the back. The partnerships you create and the connections you make will open doors to rooms of opportunities that you may not be able to open on your own. You can not be successful alone. You can try to be the owner, manager, technician, and maintenance, but you will get burnt out easily and be less productive and prosperous in doing so.

Remember me telling you about when I opened the first gym. I had the vision of how I wanted it to look, I knew what I wanted and didn't want, I knew how to train the athletes, I knew how to do the books, I knew how to manage the clients, I knew how to clean the carpets. I knew how to do all of these things, and I tried to do it ALL for a while. I had the issue of delegating and trusting that everything would get done without me having to touch it. This is when my friend, Felicia said, "People want to help you, but you won't let them." I started to slowly let go of some of the tasks and develop more of a partnership than a Sole Proprietorship. I now had a partner to assist me, support me, tell me when I was doing too much, and give the guidance to help make the business more productive and prosperous. With doing this, it allowed me to be more available to actually walk in my purpose. I had more time to prepare for classes, I had more time to rest, and I had more time to actually live when I allowed the right people in.

Positivity is important to your everyday life. If you can not find the positive in a situation, change the way you think about the situation. If you can not find a positive person on your team of people you surround yourself with, then you may need to reevaluate the people in your circle. It may be challenging at first to make the adjustments. But once you do, I promise your productivity will sky rocket with those few changes.

P- Proclamation:

The power of your proclamation means to make a clear declaration of something, especially one dealing with great importance. You would be amazed how powerful your words are to your productivity, prosperity, and purposeful living. Your words are so powerful that you can bring life or death to your situations. Words will either encourage your progress or discourage you from moving forward towards your dreams. Words that you speak about your life will make a difference in your self-motivation or self-destruction.

The words that you put in the atmosphere on a daily basis set the framework for your life. If you wake up every morning and make a declaration that you will have a productive day, your brain starts to get in alignment with your words. So, even when your day starts to derail because it will, your brain brings back the remembrance of what you said that morning that your day will be productive. In contrast, when you wake up and the first words you proclaim are that your day is going to suck; chances are, your day will suck. You will be looking for something to go wrong throughout the day, and when it goes well you will be looking for a problem to occur. This is because your brain is looking for the words that you spoke. This is the reason why meditation in the morning is very important. When you meditate and speak positive affirmations over your life, you bring into your life the energy that will help your day be positive. This is also in correlation to the Law of Attraction.

Your words send out vibrations and sound and these vibrations will create your reality that surrounds you. Remember, words are creators; the creators of your universe, your life, and your reality. Without your words, your thoughts can never become a reality. So what can you learn from this? If your words and thoughts are the very tools with which you create your reality, then surely they are our most powerful tool yet? Surely you should only proclaim the very best words in order to create your very best reality? It is your proclamation of your desires for your life that show a bold affirmation of your thoughts.

Many of you have heard the phrase to choose your words wisely. This is because of the power attached to the outcome of those words in your life. Some words have the power to inspire you to live life differently, ignite a flame in your spirit to go after what you want, and to influence your heart and minds to make a change in your life. These words have the power to uplift, encourage, and motivate yourself to live a better life like: can, will, must, got this, determined. Just like there are positive words, there are also negative words that can cause you to hesitate, turn back, or never try. These words are just as powerful because if you speak them and believe them they will cause your life to be stagnant. Words like: can't, won't, or never will, tell the universe that you are not ready for your life to go to the next level.

    I remember when I started changing my proclamations. I didn't just change it within myself, with all of my teams, in my class, and with my family. I took the word can't out of my vocabulary, and I refused to allow them to use the word in the gym, class, or the house. Whenever I had new athletes enter the gym, one of the first rules taught by myself and the other athletes was to never say the word can't. If they said this word during practice or lessons, they had to do five push-ups every everytime they said it. This was my way of training their brains and their words. In order to prepare for competitions every athlete had to have a positive mindset. So, when doing new routines, stunts, and tumbling it took everyone being on the same page believing they could because of the intricate transitions. If one athlete would say what they can't do, the team would fall apart. I explained how their words for what they could do were very powerful, and if they wanted to advance to a higher level, they would have to push past what they couldn't do at that time, but understand that with time, energy, and effort they would be able to do what they once thought they couldn't. The word can't is an automatic declaration that you won't ever be able to reach the goals you set for yourself.

    Even in class, I would be teaching new lessons, and of course, anything that you learn that is new to you will be challenging to begin with. This is what I explained, and I had several students say what they can't do because it was too hard, so they would not even try. Their actions line up with their words because when you say you can't your brain says, ok, I guess we can't; so, your actions won't try. Those students that declared what they couldn't do would have to write 10x's that they could do whatever it was that they said they couldn't do. In doing this, they are now removing the negative statements and replacing them with repetitive positive statements. So, it would look like, I can read, I can write, or I can pass this test.

    With my family, I would get on their nerves. I would correct their words whenever they would talk about what they couldn't do, or especially, if they said something about what I couldn't do. This came when I would always talk about what I was going to do in my life, especially when I set new goals that no one could see how I would accomplish them. I would always tell them that I can do whatever I put my mind to do. Which is true. Anytime, I would speak of a new goal and actually go after it with all my energy then the universe would reciprocate and reward me with my efforts. I would speak the same over their lives, but some would still speak negative words into their situations. When this would happen, it would remind me of how powerful the words you proclaim for yourself are.

Let's help you live a more productive, prosperous, and purposeful life with your words. These are a few ways to guide you in your efforts to proclaim life over your life.

-Using the words I AM:

These are two very powerful words that will affirm who you are, your dreams, your visions and your goals with the words 'I am'. Think about what you say you are, do you say: I am ugly? I am fat? I am dumb? I am lazy? I am no good? I am not worthy? I am not "fill in the blanks"? These two words are pretty small, but they are very mighty. The way you fill in the blank after the I Am will determine how you view yourself and how others will view you. Remember your words are creating your reality; therefore, even if there is no truth in what you say, the truth is being created because it is what you believe. When people fill in the blank with, I am beautiful? I am smart? I am confident? I am productive? I am prosperous? I am purposeful? You will begin to operate in more confidence in your life. You must be consistent with those words. They will saturate your spirit and your life will begin to change. You define your reality with the words of your lips.

-Control the Complaining:

How often do you complain on a daily basis? Take the time to think about how frequently a complaint comes out of your mouth. Let's think about some that most people have in common. Do you complain about work/job/career? Do you complain about your children/parents/spouse? Do you complain about your finances? Do you complain about other people and how they do what they do? Do you complain about your looks/hair/body? Do you complain about your life? Maybe, your life doesn't fit into any of these complaints. It can be something as simple as complaining about traffic, lines in a store, or how some food tastes. There is a difference between making something known or bringing an issue to the light.

These complaints may be valid in order to make something right. These are not the complaints I am speaking of. Sometimes, you have to speak up and present a complaint to others, but there is a tactful way to make a complaint. I am talking to those that find something to complain about everyday and those are the words that consistently come out of your mouth. When you complain, what do you do about what you're complaining about? If you do nothing, then you are putting negative energy in the universe for no reason, but to release your feelings about a situation. Complaining can become so common in your life that you do not realize how much you do it. This type of complaining can lead to a destructive lifestyle because if you complain about everything then what progress is being made. It is difficult to make progressive strides towards a goal if you are so focused on all the things that go wrong during the process. Usually when people are striving towards a purpose, those that consistently complain about the process, they stop and turn back because of the difficulties that come along with the process. On the other hand, those that come against challenges and don't stay focused on the complaint, change the way they speak about the challenge, and keep moving forward.

I remember as an educator during COVID, we had to teach through an online platform. I didn't have the technical skills at that moment to effectively teach virtually. I complained everyday when I woke up. I complained on my way to school. I complained when I stepped foot into the classroom. I complained to every teacher that would listen. I complained when I got home. It wasn't until my daughter said to me, what happened to the positive person she knew me to be. My complaining had become Toxic. I was finding something to complain about everyday, every change they made even if it was supposed to benefit us. I would not take the time out to accept the changes because my complaining was louder than anything they could say. My technical skills were not improving because my complaining got in the way of my learning. They were trying to teach me how to teach more effectively virtually, but I wasn't listening. I became that negative energy that filled the hallways. My complaining affected others because who really wants to be around someone that is always complaining about something. I know I didn't, but I had become that person. I wasn't doing anything to try to make the changes better, I wasn't even trying to think of ways to make it better. When she said that to me, I had to self-reflect on what I was doing with my life. I was self-destroying everything from work, students, and family with the words that I would proclaim. I had to ask myself, why am I complaining? I didn't like it and it was a challenge for me. What can I do to change the situation?

Nothing because it was the way the world was changing. The last question was, Do you like the energy you are putting out? No, So I changed my words.

You must self-reflect on the words that come out of your mouth. Becoming more self-aware is the first step to realizing how to control your complaints.

When you proclaim the desires for your life, then your thoughts, your words, and your actions will work together to bring your desires to manifestation. Remember, when you proclaim, everyone will not support you in your endeavors. This is when you can not let the power of other people's words cause you to doubt yourself.

When you start speaking about what you can do, and what you will do, some people will question your methods of how you will reach these goals, why you need or want your goals, and only show you the downfalls of what you are going after.

You must speak against these oppositions, by using words like "I don't receive them" or "Not me". So be cautious of who you proclaim your goals to. You will have some people that will support you and be in agreement with their words for your life. But please know, that when you make the proclamation, you must be bold in your beliefs of receiving. If you are not courageous in what you are proclaiming, it makes it difficult for others to support and to be in agreement with you. If you are waffling or unsure, it would be better to not speak it because it will not be spoken with boldness.

I remember when I was transitioning into Professional Speaking, and I would say in my intro that I was an Educator, Coach, and Business Owner. I would proclaim these careers boldly because I had confidence that those were what I was. When it came to proclaiming being a Motivational Speaker, I would not be bold when the words came out to tell people that I was this also. It wasn't until one of my speaking consultants said after a keynote, "You're not transitioning into a speaker. You are a speaker already so start speaking that with boldness. After I heard those words, my words changed. I boldly proclaim that " I AM a Professional Speaker."

P- Peace of Mind

Your proclamations play a major part in your peace of mind. The power of having a peace of mind will keep your life on track. Your peace of mind is a mental state of calmness or tranquility, a freedom from worry or anxiety. The feeling of being at peace with yourself and with your life. In order to gain and maintain your peace of mind, it can not be situational. It should not be contingent on your circumstances.

You must learn how to have a peace of mind when challenges arise in your life because they will. Life will throw you obstacles, so when you learn to control your peace of mind, you will not be overthrown.

Having a peace of mind will take the focus off your F.L.A.W.S. This acronym represents your Fear, Lack, Anxiety, Worries, and Stress. These flaws will keep you moving backwards. Let's address them each, one-by-one:

FEAR-

Fear is an emotion that arises based on an anticipation or awareness of a possible threat of harm or danger. The fear of the unknown is one of the most crippling emotions that hinder your life from pursuing dreams, visions, and goals. The Fear of not knowing what the outcome will be and the possibility that the pursuit will cause harm to your life. Fear creates a stronghold over your life if you allow it to control your thoughts about everything you desire to do. Fear of Failure is another type of fear that prevents dreams from manifesting. The thoughts of failing scream louder in your brain than the thoughts of succeeding. You learn how to quiet those thoughts when you focus on peace of mind.

Breathe through the fear: This will help your mind take hold of the fear and work through it calmly.

Face your Fears: Whatever your fear is, if you face it, it will begin to fade away. Your mind doesn't feel the emotion as much if the situation repeats.

Don't try to be perfect: When taking risks that are fearful, the facts are that you do not have to be perfect to start. Just start. A lot of people fear pursuing goals because they think it needs to be perfect.

Remember the scripture about, FEAR NOT.
"Fear not, for I am with you; be not dismayed, for I am your God; I will strengthen you, I will help you, I will uphold you with my righteous right hand." Isaiah 41:10

LACK-

Lack is the state of being without or not having enough. Lack can disturb your mental state of mind because it can cause anxiety, worries, and stress within your life, or it can be the motivator that fuels your drive. You can lack in many areas of your life including confidence in yourself, resources to sustain yourself, or lack of motivation. When you have a lack anywhere in your life, remember that you can
change lack into abundance. The way you view your situation is how you overcome it. In order to gain and maintain a peace of mind, is to know that whatever is lacking in the moment can be obtained. So, instead of focusing on the fact that there is something missing which causes the mind to not be at rest, you work on finding ways to create what is missing. This will work for anything you lack.

Recognize the possibilities of how to increase whatever is not enough

Practice the skills needed to improve in whichever area is lacking

Do not dwell on what you don't have, realize what you need and go after that

Remember, Lack is a temporary state that can be a stumbling block or a stepping stone, you decide how you want to view it to create your peace of mind.

ANXIETY-

Anxiety is the feeling of uneasiness, dread, or nervousness about a potential situation. It may not be dangerous and it may not have even happened, but your mind has thought about all the possible negative outcomes. This is the exact opposite of peace of mind. When dealing with anxiety, you may have trouble concentrating or thinking about anything besides the current event that is causing the immense sense of panic. If you want to achieve your dreams and goals, you must be able to control your daily activities to become more productive. When anxiety controls you, you are more hesitant to take chances on life because you may avoid certain people, places, or situations to prevent these feelings. When feeling anxious, your thoughts are going to flood your mind.

Bring it to peace by:

Visualize a Happy Place- think of places that make you happy and see it in your mind. For me it's the beach, the ocean waves, and the shining sun.
Relaxation Techniques- This could be meditation music to calm your dreadful thoughts. This will cause your heart rate to slow and body to release the tension.
Physical Routines- Being active increases the mood and wellness of our minds. Reduce the caffeinated drinks because they increase anxiety.

Remember this scripture, "Be anxious for nothing, but in everything by prayer and supplication, with thanksgiving, let your requests be made known to God; and the peace of God, which surpasses all understanding, will guard your hearts and minds through Christ Jesus" (Philippians 6-7, NKJV).

WORRY-

Worry sets in when you give way to the anxiety and you let it flow throughout your life. Worry is the act of dwelling on difficulties or troubles. It is meditating on the negative. Worrying is the uncertainty of the problems or potential problems. This is when you take the fear and anxiety about moving forward with your dreams, and you only foresee the worst that can happen. Worried about, What if I fail? What if I lose? What if I am not good enough? These what ifs pile up in the brain and build a wall of self-doubt, self-sabotage, and eventually self-hate. Because after all is said and done, those that worry so much about what will happen, in turn regret not trying in the end. Most het older and say, I wish I would have not worried so much about life and lived life.

There are ways to manage the worries and bring about peace to be productive.
Write down your Worries- Make a list of the things you worry about
Ask Yourself- "Can I do anything about this worry?"
If yes- Make a plan on how to solve the problems to stop the worrying
If no- Give yourself a small time to worry, collect these worries, and refocus them by thinking of a different outcome than the original.

Constant worrying can take a physical and emotional toll on yourself causing your mind to not function properly.

Remember this Scripture found in Matthew 6:34, "Therefore, do not worry about tomorrow, for tomorrow will worry about itself. Each day has enough trouble of its own." You may not be able to stop problems from coming in our lives, but one thing we do not have to do is worry about it.

STRESS-

Stress is the reaction when you feel under pressure, overwhelmed, or unable to cope. This can lead to physical and psychological strain. Stress can be the result of extreme worrying and can truly cause medical issues. You can not be productive if you are not properly handling the stress as it enters into your life. Anytime you experience some degree of stress, it is all in how you manage and respond. There are several types of stressors that require different responses that will determine how the stress affects your well-being.

For Instance:

-Take time for yourself/Self-Care

According to research, in order to be your best self, you need to take time for yourself. Make sure you schedule time each week for you. During this time, do what you want, relax, read, or go for a walk. That, me time, is when you actually refresh your mind and not just while you sleep.

-Practice Mindfulness as a Lifestyle

Directing all of your attention and awareness to the present. This will take

practice, but when you work towards being more mindful; it will pull you out of the negative downward spiral that can be caused by too much daily worry about things you can or cannot change.

This is when I remember the Serenity Prayer:

God grant me the serenity (peace of mind) to accept the things I can not change. The courage to change the things I can, and the wisdom to know the difference.

When something happens, you are asking for peace of mind in any situation. You must realize what you can change and what you can not change, and know the difference between both. This will be a guide to your Peace.

I remember allowing every letter in FLAWS to affect me when I dropped my daughter off at college. We flew from Houston, Texas to Atlanta, Georgia to move her into her dorm in the summer of 2022. She had never been away from home longer than a week at camps. Her and I had never been apart longer than a few days because even at camp I saw her a couple of times. Now, she was about to be away for months. It had been her and I for the past 18 years what was I supposed to do without her. The last day of Orientation they had a Parting Ceremony, they told us to hug them and leave the building. Students stayed, parents exited. I was distraught. I sobbed as I walked to the car. I cried going to the airport; I cried on the plane. My mind was full of fear and anxiety. I was worried about what would happen to my baby. I was leaving her in a city thousands of miles away. What if she had an asthma attack and no one was there to help? What if she was overwhelmed by anxiety? What if sheś alone and doesn't make any friends? I allowed every worry in the world that you can think of as a mother to enter my mind, and instead of casting my worries away, I cradled them and brought them home with me. It was one of toughest times in my life walking into my house without my daughter with me. Waking up the next morning alone was miserable. I was alone, now what am I going to do with my life? How am I going to make it without her? She had been my life. I cried the entire next day. I did not leave my house. I was a mess. I was lacking self-control, focus, motivation, and I could feel the stress infiltrating my body. There was no Peace of Mind, no Productivity, no Prosperity, and no purposeful living at that moment.

Then Sunday came, I got up, went to church, cried on the way there, cried while I was there, but heard the message. Me vs. Me. This message triggered a shift in my thoughts. It was time for a refreshing. A renewal of life, and I was stopping myself. I asked myself, why are you so sad? Why do you keep crying? Why are you so hurt? Isn't this what we prayed for? Didn´t she get exactly what she wanted? If so, why aren't you celebrating? Why are you not excited? All of these questions made me realize, it was time for me to take my life to a new level and realize that my daughter was going to be alright. I had to stop worrying about the problems that could happen and focus on the fact that she is living her dreams. She wanted to go to that school. She

worked really hard, and her hard work paid off. We got everything we had
been praying for the year before, and I had the nerve to be sad because she wasn't still with me. How dare I? It is not like she was dead, but I knew that
life would never be the same, and I had to be at peace with the decisions that we made.

After I recognized what I could and could not change, I refreshed myself; I reset my mindset; then I restarted the next week with a Peace of Mind knowing that
everything would be alright. So, when she calls with a stressful situation that causes her fear, worry, or be anxious, I remind her of the Serenity Prayer to keep a Peace of Mind and practice mindfulness. Focusing on the Present Day and preparing for tomorrow, but not worrying about it. In order for her just like you to be productive, prosperous, and purposeful, you must gain and maintain a Peace of Mind because progress can not be seen in chaos. Chaotic mind will not be stable to move forward.

P-Present Day Focus

Being present means enjoying and appreciating the life around you. There is power in focusing on the present moment. When you focus on the things you have and are grateful for what you have, you will realize that you have come through obstacles and overcome your past. A famous quote says, "If you wanna stay sad, live in the past. If you want to be anxious, keep worrying about the future, but if you want to be happy, focus on the present and be grateful. Gratitude will help you when you start to feel unproductive and you start going in the wrong direction.

Also, forgive and forget. Now this is easier said than done of course, but holding onto unforgiveness creates bitterness and prevents you from excelling to the next level. You have to be able to forgive those that have hurt you in the past and caused you any pain or trauma. If you do not, you are not able to move on into a future that is going to be more productive. I have a saying, "Get past being pissed." A lot of times, we are so upset and mad with people from the past because of what they've done, but that anger towards them actually shows when we get into other relationships with other people. We tend to not trust as much, to not open up as much, and to hurt others because of the hurt that we experienced in the past. So if you don't let the past go then the past will determine your future.

Living in the present; This goes along with forgive and forget. The past is gone and the future is yet to come, so your past you doesn't need you, your future you does. Live in the present moment so that you can make the most out of the current time that you have on Earth. The present moment should not be taken lightly. A lot of time we waste our tea, which is our time, energy, and attention on situations that cause our present to not be as joyous as it can be. Enjoy the journey of life as you go through it day by day. Learn to let go of the anxiety for the what if this and what if that about the future, and the what about when this happened from the past. The present is the moment that you can do something about, so live in it.

You can tell when you are being more present with yourself because you will start to:
-Become more aware of emotional shifts. You notice within yourself that you are allowing your emotions to take control, and you bring them under control before they do.

- Become more aware of your body. Your body will tell you when you need to take a break, either mentally or physically. You start to pay attention and make adjustments.

- Become more intentional with your time and energy. You will spend less time wrapped up in negative thoughts or moods.

When you practice being in the present moment, it doesn't mean that you are not doing anything that moves you toward your future. It means that as you are moving, you are not stressing as much, more calm, and you are knowing where you are and where you are going. You are surrounded by distractions which makes the focus on present time for challenging; however, there are some ways to enhance this powerful tool:

Appreciate life & what you have:

Be grateful for your blessings no matter what size they are, big or small. Also, no matter what life throws your way. Be grateful for what you have. When you're grateful, you'll be able and open to receive more. Its like a child, if you give a child a gift of $1, and they are appreciative of the small amount. You may be more willing to give them a larger amount later. In contrast, if they complain about the $1, you may think they are ungrateful and want to take back the $1 and never give them anything else in the future. Remember that, even in your small beginnings, be grateful.

I remember listening to Oprah talk about how she got to be so successful and prosperous in life. She said that, "We need to practice and develop the spiritual muscle that allows you to check in with yourself. Develop the clarity of your own knowing, but in order to do that we have to live in the space of gratitude." She said that this was her number one spiritual practice. She practiced being grateful and this is how she got everything that she has. So, Practice being grateful. She read a quote that stated, "Do not waste your time desiring what other people have. Remember the things you have now, are things you once desired." She explains how being grateful changes your personal vibration.

- Don't take things for granted:

A lot of times you may take people, places, what you have, or just being alive for granted. Without realizing how appreciative you should be to have the things that you have. When you start to be grateful for the things you have, it will create happiness and a more content life. Realizing that it could always be worse and that you are in a better position than before should make you realize that your perspective is what determines your thankfulness or your ungratefulness. Especially with people, you never know when you will lose someone or you will be gone yourself.

I remember telling myself never to go to bed angry at someone because you don't know if that will be the last time talking to that person. Remember, when I got sick in 2019, I went to sleep one night and was rushed to the hospital the next morning. My blood pressure dropped, my fever spiked, and I went into a Septic Shock. This is when I faded away. They brought me back. It was sudden and my life changed. I was placed in the Intensive Care Unit. I had to have multiple blood transfusions, be on an oxygen machine, heart monitoring, and daily tests to see what was causing my body to shut down.

The Sepsis was infecting my body, spreading and causing my organs to malfunction and eventually shut down. After being in the hospital a week, undergoing treatment after treatment, I never took my life or others for granted. I realized how suddenly people can be gone.

-Live your life based on your values

Values meaning what are your beliefs and boundaries. Your perspective of your values will determine what you will do and what you won't do. So you must determine what your values are, what's important to you? When you know this, you will also know what you are willing to put up with and not put up with? This is important to keep your life in balance. You are not worried about putting yourself in a compromising position because you value your life. When you don't have anything you value in life, it is easy to be distracted and swayed by others to pull you off track with where you want to be.

The benefits of being present improves your relationship with others and your ability to focus which both are required for productive and prosperous living.

P-Patience

Patience is the ability to accept or tolerate delay without getting upset or angry. Having patience means the ability to wait. The power of patience is so important when endeavoring new adventures in life. Being patient in the learning process, and being patient in the times of struggles. Patience allows you to reap the benefits in the time they are supposed to flourish. Living a life of prosperity and purpose takes patience. Everything may not come when you want it, and it may not manifest according to your timeline, but with patience and persistence your dreams and goals can and will come to pass. Just because there is a delay in receiving, does not mean that itś not meant to happen. Sometimes things need to be fully developed before it is time. It is like a harvest. If you dig up the seed before it has time to fully take root, then you will not get the desired results. An illustration is how the stalk of corn must go through the process of producing. First the blade, then the ear, then the full grain of corn on the ear. If you cut down the stalk before it´s time, then you will not get the actual kernels of corn. Therefore, patience is very important.

Some say, patience is a virtue. I always wondered what this meant and why so many people say it. I discovered that it meant it is a valuable quality for a person to not get upset while waiting. Waiting, one of the toughest things for people to do on a daily basis. People do not like to wait. Think about all of the places you have to wait: in line at the store, in traffic on freeway, or in life for manifestations. When you lack patience, you can miss out on receiving what is for you in your life. Lacking patience can cause you to give up on your dreams before they have time to fully flourish. The lack of patience causes some to lack self-control, get annoyed easily, lash out and complain. When you're being patient, you'll stop and take a moment to look around while thinking about the bigger picture. That is, you won't just think about your actions in the present moment but what they'll mean down the road, too. Patience pays off even though it may be difficult at the moment.

If your patience level is not very high, you can increase the amount of patience you have. It takes time, and to become extremely patient takes a lot of willpower.

Having the power over your need for instant gratification teaches you self-control and regulates your emotions. Demonstrating patience will increase collaboration, creativity, and even productivity. When working with others you will not always get what you want from them when you want it. The process may take others longer to figure it out while you may get it very quickly. This is something that I have grown to learn over my years of working with people in the service field as manager or public service as an educator.

I remember struggling with the ability to be patient. While attending the Bible training institute, I had to do a research project. We had to pull different traits from the bible and of course, patience was mine. During my research, I had to also practice the skill of being patient. I was not very good at all. This was during the time when my patience was at itś worst. In the management field, we are compensated for monetary growth and in order to grow we had to be efficient and effective. As the manager it is our responsibility to produce results, and by any means possible sometimes. I managed every team in the store from Stock Replenishment to Department Managers.

Everything had to move according to the timeframe I put in place and the flow had to be impeccable. I did not have time for any delays with our shipments. I did not have time for any merchandise problems, and I especially did not have the time nor the patience to deal with employee issues. This made me a very cold and uncompassionate manager. My patience was as short as a second. I did not put up with inferiority. I was always angry at someone, always screaming at some associate, it was never done the way I wanted it. These were some pretty ugly times for me. In order to pass the assignment, I had to demonstrate the skill on a daily basis to learn and grow. It was so difficult to not be in control. It was so difficult to sit back and wait for tasks to get done. I had to still do my job, but do it without the agitation or frustration that I would show. I did a lot of walking away and deep breathing exercises; instead of screaming and upsetting my associates. This took them by surprise. When I told them, I was practicing patience and they would all burst out in laughter. Then they noticed that I wasn´t down their backs as much, and I was patiently waiting on days where I would usually be frantic. I found them getting the job down but without all of the stress that I would be in the situation. My tolerance levels grew and my stress levels declined, all because of the power of having patience. Without it, I was headed towards a cycle of being hated by those that I asked to do the most for me.

I remember I did the paper for the project and I used Job as my character. If you are unaware of who Job is, hereś a quick synopsis.

Job was a faithful man and had everything he wanted; when one day, it was all taken away. He lost his family, friends, livestock, fortunes, and his health. His wife told him to curse God and die. But no, Job waited patiently to be restored. He did not walk around complaining about his situation. He did not engage in the madness that some were telling him to do. In Job's patience, he ended up being alone. I would think about how someone can go from having everything to nothing and not be upset. But in the end, after waiting and going through trials and tribulations; he regained it all. He was restored with everything and double. In my paper, I focused on the end results and how he got more than what he had, but if he would have complained, cursed God, or decided to follow his friends, chances are he would have never received what God had for him. His patience paid off in the long-run.

    Remember, don't stress when there is a delay or when things don't go your way. Sometimes you are not prepared for what God has for you. You are blessed in the timing that you are prepared for. Imagine if you received your million dollars today, what would you do with it? Would you know how to invest it, or would you spend it all up and before you know it you are broke. We sometimes want these blessings out of timing. You don't want to be swallowed up by what comes with it. You will receive everything that you desire and deserve, but be patient and you will obtain without the strain of maintaining.

    Remember when I told you, I wanted to be married. If I would have gotten married the few times I was engaged, I would be divorced by now, I'm sure. I was not ready to be a wife at 21 the first time I was engaged or at 24 the second time I was engaged. I had not prepared to do what a wife needed to do for her husband and for her family. I had not even lived my own life. Then when I was proposed to at the age of 30, I knew not to even accept the ring. I was on the corporate climb of my career and marriage was not even a thought. I thought about the big wedding and beautiful dress, but I was not ready for everything else that came with being married. So, now that my life has evolved and I have grown up. I am now patiently waiting for the right man to be a part of my life. This takes patience because I could go out right now and find a man to marry, but would it be the right thing to do? NO. My patience in waiting is going to reward me with the King that God has been preparing for me and set aside for me. I believe I will be like Job in this situation, I will be blessed with more than what I could ever expect from my husband because I patiently waited.

There is power in your patience. The power to withstand difficult situations and not lose your peace of mind. The ability to have a divine delay that may save your life. I always believe that a delay is not always bad. Delays can be intervals in life that keep you from going through obstacles that could make your life worse. Like think about the time when, you may not have been able to find your keys when you were in a hurry to leave somewhere. Then you find them after 5 minutes of searching, get on the road in a rush, and find yourself stuck in traffic because of a wreck that happened five minutes prior to you being on that same highway. Those small delays can be divine interventions that lead to better situations. The times when you think you have been overlooked for promotions or opportunities then you see the stress and burden that the position you wanted has on the person that actually got it. At that moment is when you are thankful that it wasn't you having to endure the burdens. Then another position is made available to you that is better for you.

However, in your times of delay, waiting patiently doesn't mean to not do anything.

You are still working towards your goals, but with a positive attitude and not begrudgingly. For example, me waiting for my husband. I am not just sitting around waiting, and not making myself available to be seen. I am preparing myself to be a "good wife", as they say. I am working on being a better me, so when my partner finds me, he finds a good thing, not just a woman waiting to be completed by him. You still put in the work while you wait. While you wait for your business to flourish, you continue doing what it takes to make it grow. While you wait patiently for your prosperity to manifest, you keep sowing seeds that will reap the harvest you desire.

While you are patiently waiting to know that you are fulfilling your purpose, you continue walking in it until you see the pay off.

P-Perseverance

The Power of Perseverance or persistence in the face of adversity. Despite the difficulties, despite the failures, despite the oppositions, you continue to persevere to achieve the success you desire for your life. You want to be productive, prosperous, and purposeful, these won't come if you give up. Perseverance is never giving up when the going gets tough. The only guarantee that you won't succeed and it will never happen is when you give up. Giving up is the guarantee that you will never achieve the dreams you desire.

There are so many people in this world that have become successful and achieved their goals, but they had so many obstacles that got in their way. Most of the celebrities you may know past and present had to overcome life. They had to push past all of the stumbling blocks that they faced. The many doors that were closed in their faces. The many rejections that they received. I could not count the number of No´s that every famous person heard before they were famous. Not just celebrities, what about business owners, inventors, or authors. Do you know how many times an inventor has to fail before the invention actually works. It takes multiple failures and only one time to work. In order to get a book published, an author must hear how many times that it´s not good enough before one person says yes it is. It only takes one to say yes, no matter how many noś you receive. How many Noś can you hear before you will stop pursuing your dreams? Do you have a number, or is the answer until you hear a yes?

I remember teaching a lesson to the students about never giving up. During this lesson, I give them 12 famous people, and 12 failures. They had to match the person to the failure. Every class would be shocked to know some of the backstories behind the people that they only saw as successful. One of the famous authors included J.K. Rowling, many students knew her from her fame with Harry Potter, but they had no idea that before her fame she lived on government assistance as a single mom. She fought through poverty and depression, after her divorce. It was on a delayed train that she discovered the idea of Harry Potter, but it wasn´t until seven years later it became a book, and even then the book was rejected by up to twelve publishers. As I told her story to the class, I kept asking them, how many noś could they take.

J.K. Rowling is a great example of perseverance, but sheś not alone.

As I gave example after example , they began to see the pattern.
- For example, Lionel Messi, everyone in class knew who he was. They knew him as a famous soccer player that had won many championships, and he was one of the highest paid athletes in the world. But they did not know at the age of 11, he was diagnosed with a growth hormone deficiency that caused extreme medical expenses and he had to undergo treatments at such a young age. Messi did not let his health deter him from his dreams.

-Oprah Winfrey- Famous Talk show host, TV Network Owner, Actress, Magazine and Book Creator, Multi-Billionaire, Motivational Speaker had to overcome adversity her entire life. We know her for what she is now, but she was fired from her job as a news anchor because they didn't like her look. Guess what, instead of giving up, she found a different avenue to pursue her purpose. She created her personal brand of Oprah and persevered to become one of the most prominent personalities in the world.

- When I told them about Steve Jobs, they almost lost their minds. Continuously asking, how can you fire the co-founder? They all know him for his innovation of Iphones and Ipads. Yes, Steve Jobs- Co-Founder and creator of Apple Products, Multi-Millionaire was dismissed from his position at Apple in 1985. I always ask, how do you get fired from a company that you helped create? He took his wealth of knowledge and innovation and started a different company until Apple came calling him back. He persevered even when the people he helped become who they were didn´t see his vision.

- I couldn't leave out the ever so popular,Michael Jordan- Famous NBA Basketball player, led his Chicago Bulls to six Championships, and the creator of the JORDAN brand, was rejected from his basketball team in high school because he wasn't good enough. He didn't let the rejection stop him from pursuing his basketball career. He practiced longer and harder, he got stronger and smarter. He never gave up. Persevering through pain, trauma, and heart-ache as he grew his brand bigger and better. He did not let what one person told him stop him.

What about you? What dreams, visions, and goals do you have for your life that you have been told no to. Did you hear the one no and believe them? Did you sit your dreams on the shelf because you couldn't see past the person that laughed at your dreams. Well it is time to pick them back up. When someone says no, ask them how it could be improved in their opinion, and again this is someoneś opinion. It does not make it facts. If itś a business idea, listen to the suggestions, if they line up with your goals, make the adjustments. If you are not as skilled in what you are trying to be, work on improving your skills, don't just take the no, and not work to improve.

Perseverance is about continuing to put forth the effort to obtain your goals. The saying says, ´When the tough get going, the going gets tough¨. So you can not expect there to be no resistance. It is like driving a car. As long as the car is sitting there there is nothing pushing against it, but once it gets going, you have the wind and sometimes roadblocks that cause you to detour. The going may get tough, but if you remain tough while on your road to success you will get to your destination.

Imagine yourself in a pool. When you first enter the pool, it is shallow and calm. If you just sit still near the steps, the chances of drowning are slim. It is when you decide you want to make it to the other side of the pool instead of just sitting on the steps. As you stand, you will begin to see some ripples in the water, but you can still feel the ground. The first few steps you take create bigger and more frequent ripples. This causes your legs to work a little harder because you now have the resistance of the water pressing against you, but you are okay because you can still feel the ground. You stop for a moment and take a look back, you have the choice to return to the steps from where you started or continue towards your goal to reach the other side. Now, it would be much easier to return to where you came from. It was much safer, but you will never get to your destination if you turn around now. So, you continue to take a few more steps. Now, the pool is getting deeper, and you are getting further away from your comfort zone. You begin to experience stronger waves pushing against your body, and your body is becoming more submerged in the water. You are closer to reaching your goal, but your legs are going to have to work a lot harder to push through. Now all of the doubts start to flood your mind. Should you have taken the risks? Would you make it? Would you drown? Should you take these next steps or should you turn around? The decisions to make while you are in the midst of your struggles. But you aren't even struggling yet, you can still touch the ground, and you can see the end of the pool ahead. You decide to persevere because you know that getting to the other side will give you the joy you truly want and the feeling of accomplishing your goals. So, you take a few more steps, now your head is barely above water and you are on your tip-toes trying to stay above water. You are now succumbing to the pressures of the waves and the resistance of the power of the water. Your legs struggle to move, you feel the bottom of the pool and you push your body up and forward. You are back above water temporarily. You go back under, you feel the ground and you push your body back up, as you continue to go through this process a couple more times. You realize that you are closer than you thought. All you have to do is push yourself up one more time and reach out your arms, and you will make it.

This is what persevering feels like. You take the chance to pursue your dreams, it may start off as a shallow thought and emerge into a space that you have never journeyed into before. You keep going knowing that you will make it to the other side. You keep pushing yourself up when the people you thought would support you don´t. You keep pushing yourself up when the doors are closed in your face. You keep pushing yourself up and keep your eyes on the prize for what you know is yours and that you deserve. You keep pushing because most of the time you are closer than you know. Many times people give up and turn around right before their big break. They get tired;They get weary. This is when your perseverance kicks in. When you keep going even though you are tired, you will get tired of the rejections, you will get tired of continuing to push, you may need to take a pause. Take a pause but don't make it a period. Only the strong survive is such a true statement. Because if you are weak, you will give up as soon as the first wave hits. Weak people can not sustain the pressure of life. When you go after your dreams, you must be strong in your beliefs, strong in your desire, and strong in your determination. The most successful people had to be strong in pushing past the noise that would tell them to give up. If you can believe it, you can achieve it and that is not just a cliche saying. The problem with the saying is that people believe it, they try, they fail, they quit, so then they say it is not true. How do you succeed unless you fail? How do you get stronger unless you add more weight to build your muscles. How do you build endurance unless you are tested? I can attest to this.

Perseverance is something that I have learned to master. Whatever goal or dream I set my mind to achieve, when I truly go after it, I achieve it even after being tested.

I remember going through some of the most trying times in my life. My 2022 was a beast. This means that it tested me in almost every way possible from the beginning until the end. Starting in January, I had decided that I would transition careers and step into the motivational speaking arena. I went to the doctor for an annual exam like usual, and it flipped my world upside down. The doctor called back and told me that my lab results were abnormal. They showed that my blood count was six percent and the normal count was between twelve to thirteen percent. I was living on half a tank of blood. She insisted that I immediately take action before further damage was done to my body. I had become Anemic because of the low blood count causing my iron levels to be low. I was functioning on a two percent iron saturation meaning that my energy was depleted. Normal iron levels were thirty -five to forty-five percent. Now, how was I supposed to be a speaker traveling the world and my body was falling apart.

In February, I fell into a state of depression, I was in constant pain, still losing blood, and feeling weaker as the days progressed. I could tell I was dying. The doctors scheduled me to see a Hematologist who is a blood doctor. This doctor then scheduled the blood transfusions for March. It all began, the constant doctor visits, being poked and prodded. I believe I was stuck with so many needles during this time, I could not see a needle for the rest of my life. I got the transfusion in March and then to the next test because the blood was not holding, and I was losing blood on a constant basis. Next, to the Oncologist, this is the Cancer Doctor. He scheduled appointments to check my stomach, colon, and internal organs to see if they were the cause. More tests, more labs, more appointments, and more money, the medical expenses started to add up. I learned how insurance worked this year. I was paying out of pocket even though I had insurance. I have now maxed out my credit cards on just trying to find out what was wrong. I wanted to give up. I wanted to say screw it all, just let me die, but my purpose in this world is bigger than my emotions. I wanted to live for my daughter because I hadn't mentioned that this was her Senior year of High School, and I couldn´t die and leave her all alone. So, I persevered.

April came and the world seemed to be crumbling around me, my daughterś eighteenth birthday, two proms, and college visits. I was still weak, losing blood, in and out of doctors offices. I had to be strong for her and not let my struggles affect her dreams and goals. Needless to say, it was a very busy month. The first week she had dance shows that I had to show up for, Senior pictures to pay for, birthday celebrations. The end of the month she had her prom to attend on the Friday, her boyfriend´s because he was at a different school on the Saturday. Then, the next day, we boarded a plan that Sunday for Atlanta, to attend college visitations that were planned by the schools. As soon as I returned, I had Urology tests of the bladder and kidneys. I believe they tested every organ in my body, and this is when they decided I needed to have surgery. Since, they could not find any other places in my body from which I could be losing blood, they finalized the results that the massive Uterine Fibroids that had been causing me so much pain and trouble had to come out. They also determined that it was too massive to do Laparoscopic surgery. No, they had to do abdominal surgery and cut me open to take out my entire uterus. This was one of the toughest decisions to make. Undergo a major surgery that would take away my womanhood, or continue to suffer in pain and die slowly each day. I made the decision to undergo the surgery.

Another obstacle in life that would spin my life in a world wind. They wanted to schedule it for May, the next month, the month of my daughter's graduation. I was upset, confused, I didn't know what to do.

They scheduled it for the first week of May, and I prayed that I would be able to attend graduation the last week of May. I got a call and had to postpone the surgery because I had to go through pre-surgery tests and procedures.

This is when they decided that I needed to do IV Iron Infusions into my blood. I had to visit the clinics every other day and sit with an IV embedded in my arms for hours as the iron was pumped into my veins. Surrounded by patients with cancer and other medical issues, I began to feel down and think about my life on a different level. I had been complaining and acting like life was over everytime I stepped foot into the building. As I looked around the room, I could see sitting in the other chairs the many others that had it worse than me, some getting chemotherapy, some getting dialysis, and Im just getting some iron for my energy levels. I felt a sense of shame. Shame for my thoughts that had caused me to doubt whether life was worth living. As I thought about the perspective I had on my life, I began to change the way I viewed myself. I started to think of this surgery and these visits as a way to sustain my life and to make it healthier than it had been before.

I wanted to live and not just for my daughter, but for myself. I wanted to continue striving for the goals that I had set in January before I got the diagnosis. I wanted to live a productive, prosperous, and purposeful life.

My daughter graduated and I finished my last IV Infusion in June. This is when I met a group of people that would help me persevere to the next level. I started attending meetings that taught me how to build my speaking business and taught me how to make money in the process. I would listen, ask questions, and soak it all in. I stopped thinking about how tough life had been and started thinking about how great life can be. I learned so much in this one month about technology and networked with like-minded people. This is when my dreams began to manifest. During a meeting, they explained how to set-up a Podcast. This was one of my goals on my vision board from January. I had the vision and dream to start a weekly podcast that would shed light on what people have been going through in their lives and how they overcame it. It was a vision that one of my students gave me during my trials and tribulations earlier that school year. I decided to stop procrastinating and begin my podcast. My first one aired in the beginning of July.

July 18th, the new scheduled date for the surgery. I was down for a full Abdominal Hysterectomy where they would remove all of my female organs preventing me from bearing children or monthly pain. I had just got the momentum going for my Podcasts. I had multiple guests before entering the hospital. I entered on a Monday morning, and what was supposed to be a one night stay turned into almost a week. I thought I would be home in time for my first keynote speech, but I wasn't released and ended up doing my first keynote with this organization from a hospital bed. Talk about perseverance. I did not want to miss my opportunity to speak since this was another one of my goals on my vision board. I presented my keynote with fortitude and grace. The title was "Pressing through the Pain", and I pressed through. I had I.V.ś hooked to me, oxygen tubes, and pain medicine flowing through me. I will never forget that moment that I persevered to achieve my goals.

Doctors ordered no walking, no driving, no lifting, no long trips for six weeks at least. I could rupture my sutures and cause internal bleeding, but what they didn't know, I had a daughter going away to college in three weeks following surgery. I could not miss this for the world. Her college was 5 states away. I had to help her move into her dorm and get situated. In my heart, she could not do this without me, and I refused to let her do it without me.

Decision time again, how to get her there, how to move her in, I couldn't do it by myself. So, we decided to fly to Atlanta and have all of her items shipped.

Of course, this equaled more money. The trip had to be approved by my doctor and I had to be extremely careful. I got her moved in with the help of a friend and made her transition a lot smoother. You know what I did, I persevered. Through the obstacles that I faced whether in my health, wealth, or with my family, I did not give up. I refuse to quit in the face of adversity.

When September rolled around, I went back to teaching and felt a sense of theirs more out there for me. I decided to register for more speaking opportunities. I auditioned to be a speaker for the Successfest, a conference with hundreds of motivational speakers. I was invited to speak and this began my next phase of reaching my goals. I was a lot deeper in unfamiliar territory, but I began to gain more knowledge and courage of speaking. I enlarged my Social Media platform and started posting daily inspirational messages to encourage others to follow their dreams. I had started my Youtube channel years prior, but I never utilized it for what it was worth. When I did, my subscribers started to grow and my reach started to expand. Again, achieving goals that were on my vision board from January.

The best month of the year was upon us, October. Of course, this was the month I was born in, so I wanted October to be special. Unfortunately, I had a follow-up doctor appointment to review my progress from surgery. Was my blood holding, had the iron injections worked, was everything from surgery going back as needed. The lab results showed my iron still low and other numbers were off. I was devastated. I did not expect to hear this. I expected everything to be okay, but No. They asked if I wanted the injections again or pills to bring up my numbers. I settled for the pills. I was tired of seeing needles every time I had labs done. They had to draw blood requiring to be stuck. I was tired of going in and out of doctor's offices. I had persevered this entire year. My daughter was off at college, my career was taking flight, and I had succeeded in achieving my goals for that year, I had overcome so many obstacles already. My best month had me questioning my next moves. I wanted to quit; I wanted to throw in the towel.

November rolls around, and it reminds me of how thankful I need to be just to be alive. Living and moving with no pain for the past few months. After all I had been through, how could I give up now. Giving up wasn't an option, pressing forward was the only option. Pressing toward the mark of a higher calling. I was called to go higher in my life. I was still in the daily meeting classes and one day my mentor was teaching about how to get your name out there more. How to add more visibility to your brand, and I asked the question, what if you don't have a book to promote to push your brand? And his answer to me was, Write one. Simple as that. Write one. He made it seem so easy when he said it, then he gave me the blueprint for how to get it done. There it was, my next goal in life was to write a book. It was always a desire of mine and I knew it was part of my purpose in life.

I filled any extra time between school, games, meetings, and church, I was writing. I was researching. I was determined to achieve this goal no matter what obstacles I faced. I had the know-how all along, but I just didn't know how to get it done. Sometimes all we need is a little push in the right direction to achieve the visions, dreams, and goals that we have in our lives. Perseverance is a very powerful part of my life. I have learned to keep going even when I want to quit. I have to remember everything I do is bigger than me. My goals have to be bigger than my temporary emotions. I have to keep pushing because I know when I do, greater is on the other side of the push.

So remember, the power of persevering through situations that seem uncertain, challenging, or tough. Anything worth having is worth working for to achieve it.

Sometimes when you get what you want easily, you don't appreciate it as much. On the other hand, when you have to fight some battles to win, it's much sweeter.

When I did my first podcast interview, I felt on top of the world. I had to push through the self-doubt and my sabotage to finally do what I said I wanted to do.

Power of Prayer

Prayer is a universal and timeless act of communication with a higher power. It has the power to transform lives and bring comfort to the soul. The practice of prayer has been around for centuries, and its power has been acknowledged by people of all cultures, religions, and beliefs.

One of the most remarkable aspects of prayer is its ability to bring people together. Whether you are praying alone or with a group, the act of prayer creates a sense of unity and solidarity. When people pray together, they connect with one another on a deep level and experience a shared sense of purpose. This is why prayer is often used as a tool for healing, both physically and emotionally.

I remember being sick with a throbbing headache. As I lay in the bed, the pounding increased. I lie there praying for my head to stop hurting. The thing about prayer is that when you pray you must actually believe that your prayers will work in your life. I repeated the words over and over until my headache went away. Prayer has healing power which makes it so powerful. When you pray about your life and the situations that occur, you activate the power within the Universe to change your life and your situation. Your belief in the prayer is what causes your mind and emotions to be at rest.

Prayer has been scientifically proven to have a positive impact on mental and physical health. Research has shown that people who pray regularly experience lower levels of stress, anxiety, and depression, as well as improved sleep and better physical health. This is likely because prayer creates a sense of peace and calm in the mind and body, which can have a positive effect on overall health.

Prayer is also a powerful tool for personal growth and transformation. When you pray, you are opening yourself up to the guidance and wisdom of a higher power. This allows you to gain a new perspective on life, and to see things in a new light.

Additionally, prayer can help you gain clarity and direction in your life, which can lead to greater personal growth and fulfillment.

Finally, prayer is a means of expressing gratitude and thanks. When you pray, you are acknowledging the many blessings in your life and expressing gratitude for all that you have. This is a powerful way to cultivate a positive attitude and to increase feelings of happiness and well-being.

In conclusion, the power of prayer is truly remarkable. Whether you are seeking comfort, healing, growth, or simply a sense of connection with something greater than yourself, prayer has the power to transform your life. By making prayer a part of your daily routine, you can tap into this powerful source of strength and wisdom, and experience the many benefits that it has to offer.

Productive, Prosperous, Purposeful Living

It is not easy living a life that is consistently productive, prosperous, and purposeful. It takes work and effort on a daily basis. These ten P´s will help make your journey towards living a better life a lot more simple. If you noticed that each P has itś own definition however, many ways to increase are along the same lines. When you begin to change one of these characteristics others will slowly evolve with them. There is power in everything you do and when you realize the power you have to control your own life, and your own destiny you will be unstoppable.

Remember, Productivity is all about measuring your actions. If you are acting in a way that doesn´t direct you towards your goals, then are you being productive. This does not mean that you should not do things unproductive sometimes, but remember the more unproductive you are, the more time it will take to reach your goals. Like in the pool, if you waste time turning back and worrying, those thoughts are slowing you down from accomplishing your dreams.

Prosperity comes when productivity begins. You start your journey to prosperity once your actions fall in line with your thoughts. You can believe in being prosperous, but if you continue operating in an unproductive manner then your prosperity will be delayed. I could have been thriving as a podcaster, but my actions slowed down my progress. Prosperity follows excellence. When you operate in excellence, people will be drawn to work with you and for you. When you are unproductive, people tend to not want to help you out. Remember, prosperity isn't only about money. You can be prosperous in your health, wealth, family, and life.

Purposefully Living does not mean you know your purpose in life. You can live life with purpose and intentions on a daily basis. You would focus your actions on certain topics or people. My daughter was my purpose at one time, but she was not my purpose in life. I lived differently after having her because I had a reason to live.

When faced with difficult choices, when you live purposefully you make your choices a little more wisely. This is why discovering your purpose, increasing your patience, and obtaining a peace of mind are so powerful. They help you stay grounded when life throws fiery darts your way.

Living life can be so tiresome. I hope that the POWER of the Pś helps you live life a little less drained. The words are made to inspire you to live at another level of life, ignite a spark that motivates movement in your life, and to influence you to make the changes and take the chances that you have always dreamed of.